CONTENTS

04 WAYNE ROONEY
08 10 THINGS – LIONEL MESSI
10 PUZZLES
12 10 THINGS – SAMIR NASRI
14 ONES TO WATCH
16 ONES TO WATCH SPECIAL: TOM CLEVERLEY
18 GAFFER TAPES
20 WORLD CUP 2010: SPAIN REIGN
22 WORLD CUP ENGLAND CAPTAINS
24 SHOOT WORLD CUP AWARDS
26 WORLD CUP 2010 FACTS
28 TEN WORLD CUP 2010 MEMORIES
32 SPOT THE BOSS
34 10 THINGS – PARK JI-SUNG
36 PLAYERS' FAVOURITES
38 TEST YOUR FOOTIE KNOWLEDGE
40 YOU WHAT?
42 COMPLIMENTS OF THE SEASON
46 TOP TRIVIA
48 A-Z FOOTBALL QUIZ
52 10 THINGS – PETER CROUCH
54 SPOT THE BALL
56 PREMIER LEAGUE SECRETS
58 WHOSE PET?
59 YOUR PREMIER LEAGUE GUIDE
100 CHELSEA CHAMPIONS!
102 CHAMPIONSHIP CHAMPIONS: NEWCASTLE
104 LEAGUE 1 AND 2 CHAMPIONS: NORWICH AND NOTTS COUNTY
106 10 THINGS – JAMES MILNER
108 FUNNY PICTURES
110 ANSWERS

Pedigree

Published by Pedigree Books Ltd.
Published 2010.
PEDIGREE BOOKS, BEECH HILL HOUSE,
WALNUT GARDENS, EXETER, DEVON EX4 4DH
shoot@pedigreegroup.co.uk

EDITOR COLIN MITCHELL   **DESIGN** STUART BIRTLES
EDITORIAL ASSISTANCE LEE PRICE

> "I played against Wayne when he was 11. He bullied people with his strength and beat them with his ability. Everyone knew even then he was going to be a phenomenal player. He has just gone on and done it."
>
> **JAMES MILNER: Aston Villa and England's livewire midfielder**

> "Wayne is a class act. It was only a matter of time before he started to score more. Now he has much more and includes scoring goals rather than just supplying them. And he is a good lad."
>
> **DAVID JAMES: veteran England keeper**

> "He has taken his game to a different level. He has incredible energy and doesn't look like he gets tired. I don't know if he is stoppable."
>
> **GABBY AGBONLAHOR: speedy Aston Villa and England striker**

ROOMARKABLE!

EVERYONE AGREES WAYNE ROONEY IS STILL ONE OF THE BEST PLAYERS AROUND - DESPITE WORLD CUP 2010

"Wayne is still developing, he is only going to get better. He is a great player to have in your team. Even if he is not playing well he causes problems for the other team. He has developed his game so that he is now a goalscorer as well as joining in with overall play."
RYAN GIGGS: Wayne's Man United team-mate

"He can handle all the comments, all the praise and all of the criticism. He has been around a long time and has the experience really of a 30-year-old. He looks dangerous every time he goes on to the pitch and can score lots of goals."
GARY NEVILLE: Manchester United's veteran right-back and captain

WAYNE'S WORLD
Key dates in the ace striker's life

October 24, 1985:
Born in Liverpool

August 17, 2002:
Made his Everton debut v Spurs

October 19, 2002:
First Premier League goal v Arsenal

February 12, 2003:
First England game v Australia

September 6, 2003:
First England goal v Macedonia

August 31, 2004:
Transferred to Man United for £25.6m

September 28, 2004:
Hat-trick, United debut v Fenerbache

November 14, 2009:
Captains his country v Brazil

Where he wants to play

"My best position in any team is up front, as a forward you have to be selfish to score goals. It is a team game though and I love helping the team. I have no worries about burning out like some players who started early – just look at Ryan Giggs, he began at 16 and won the PFA Player of the Year at 35."

WAYNE'S WORDS

Wayne Rooney enjoyed his best season so far in 2009-10 with 26 Premier League goals and a whole series of blistering performances that took his game to a new level. Here's what he thinks about his goal-scoring record, his ability and football in general...

His love of football

"I dream as much as ever. If I wasn't playing for United I think I would be playing Sunday League with my mates because I just love football. I watch it on TV and if I miss a game I will watch the recording."

Taking penalties

"I always think it is important that your centre forward takes one in shoot-outs. I don't think it's a pressure you should put on defenders."

Good team-mates

"I'm playing with older players who have a lot of experience and they help me blend in. I'm quite a relaxed and shy person off the pitch but I know I am a privileged person who plays for the biggest club in the game and am doing what I love."

Scoring headers in 2009-10

"I've never really scored many goals in the air before. I am not the tallest so even when I was younger I didn't get many chances with my head. The delivery has been good for me and it's also helped that I've played up front in every game. I work on it a lot in training – timing and movement in the box, trying to get in between defenders."

Working hard

"I have always been allowed to attack players. The manager never stops you from doing that and trying to create things in the opposition half. When you score goals you get a bit more confident and I might have to get a bit more selfish in front of goal – although I will always put in the effort for the team. I think the fans appreciate a player who gives his all for the club."

10

1. Messi was the 2009 World and European Footballer of the Year. He was the first Argentine to win the Ballon D'Or, the European title.

2. When he made his league debut for Barcelona at the age of 17 years and 114 days in 2004, he was the club's third youngest-ever player in La Liga.

3. On May1, 2005, at the age of 17 years, 10 months and 7 days, Leo scored against Albacete to become Barca's youngest-ever scorer in La Liga.

4. For season 2008-09, Messi took over the No.10 shirt that had been worn by Ronaldinho before his departure to AC Milan.

5. He came on a substitute against Racing Santander on February 1, 2009, and scored two goals, the second a winner and his club's 5,000th in league football.

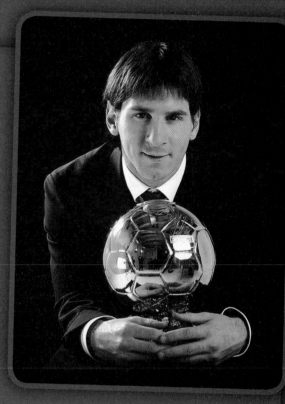

6. That same season he was the top scorer in the Champions League - and the youngest-ever to lift that award - with nine goals.

7. Messi earns around £570,000 a week - or if you want it in an even more staggering figure, around £1 every second! That makes him the world's best-paid footballer.

8. He has a buy-out clause in his contract at the Nou Camp - but it would cost you a staggering £250m if you fancied signing him!

9. In 2009, Barca extended Messi's contract to keep him with them until 2016, when he will be 28 and possibly at the height of his career!

10. Boot manufacturers went to court in a battle to get him to wear their boots - he now wears adidas and reportedly gets almost £3m a year from the deal!

PLANET FOOTBALL

WE JUST HAD THE WORLD
CUP FINALS IN SOUTH
AFRICA WITH MOST
OF THE PLANET'S TOP
PLAYERS ON SHOW.

BUT DO YOU KNOW WHERE THEY ALL
COME FROM? CAN YOU PINPOINT THEIR
HOME COUNTRIES ON A MAP OF THE
GLOBE? WE'VE GIVEN YOU A BIT OF A
HAND BY SHADING IN THE COUNTRIES
THAT MATCH THE PLAYERS TO THE RIGHT
- BUT YOU HAVE TO SEND THEM HOME!

 Samuel Eto'o
CAMEROON

 Kaka
BRAZIL

 Ryan Nelsen
NEW ZEALAND

 Park Ji-Sung
SOUTH KOREA

FAMOUS SHIRTS

SOME PLAYERS HAVE A FAVOURITE SHIRT NUMBER.

AND WHEN THEY RETIRE OR MOVE CLUBS THOSE NUMBERS LIVE ON AS LEGENDARY IN THE EYES OF FANS. CAN YOU MATCH THESE NUMBERS TO THE PLAYERS WHO HAVE WORN OR DO STILL WEAR THEM?

(7) (9) (10) (14) (23) (39)

 Thierry Henry
FRANCE — C ✓

 Gianluigi Buffon
ITALY — F ✓

 Lionel Messi
ARGENTINA — B ✓

Wilson Palacios
HONDURAS — A ✓

Alan Shearer	9 ✓
Diego Maradona	✓
Thierry Henry	
Eric Cantona	7
David Beckham	
Nicolas Anelka	39 ✓

THINGS YOU NEED TO KNOW ABOUT...
SAMIR NASRI

1. Nasri was just nine-years-old when he was signed by French giants Marseille and worked his way through the ranks to play more than 160 games for them.

2. By the time he was 20, Nasri had played over 100 games for Marseille and the club dedicated a whole day to him – including special programmes on their television channel!

3. He was transferred to Arsenal in summer 2008 for around £15m and was hailed by many as the "new Zinedine Zidane".

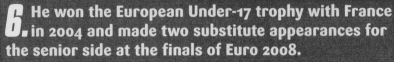

4. Samir has played for France at all levels from Under-16 and made his senior debut in March 2007 at the age of 19 when he helped set up a win against Austria.

5. His first goal for Les Bleus came on June 6, 2007, the winner against Georgia in a Euro 2008 qualifier.

6. He won the European Under-17 trophy with France in 2004 and made two substitute appearances for the senior side at the finals of Euro 2008.

7. A broken leg held up his start to season 2009-10 by two months, but once he was fit he was one of Arsenal boss Arsene Wenger's first names on the team-sheet.

8. Just before moving to The Emirates Stadium he was named the French League's Young Player of the Year and in the Team of the Season. He was also Marseille's Player of the Year in 2007.

9. Wenger rates his midfielder highly and says "He is a very intelligent boy, a quiet boy. He analyses what is happening on the pitch very quickly. He has good technical potential. He is very versatile too. He can play defensive midfield, attacking midfield and on the flanks."

10. Although he is playing among some seasoned internationals at Arsenal, Nasri began his career at Marseille playing alongside France stars Franck Ribery and Djibril Cisse.

IT'S A FACT…

Name:
Samir Nasri

Birth Date:
June 26, 1987

Birth Place:
Marseille, France

Position:
Midfielder

Clubs:
Marseille, Arsenal

Arsenal

ONES TO WATCH

GYLFI SIGURDSSON
Reading

POSITION: MIDFIELDER
DATE OF BIRTH: SEPTEMBER 9, 1989
PLACE OF BIRTH: REYKJAVIK, ICELAND
INTERNATIONAL: ICELAND UNDER-21

The Icelander joined Reading Academy in 2005 and has been out on loan at both Shrewsbury and Crewe in recent years – but last season his form caught the attention of a number of clubs.

Sigi scored his first league goal for the Royals in September last year and was named the Championship Player of the Month for March, thanks mainly to five goals in six games.

Newly promoted West Brom, plus Wolves and Bolton have been linked with the star but the management at the Madejski Stadium say they do not want to sell.

JAMES McCARTHY
Wigan

POSITION: MIDFIELDER
DATE OF BIRTH: NOVEMBER 12, 1990
PLACE OF BIRTH: GLASGOW
INTERNATIONAL: IRELAND UNDER-21

Established himself in the Wigan team last campaign and sparked an international war between the sides wanting him to play for them! Although he has turned out for the Republic of Ireland at under-17, 18, 19 and 21 levels, he was eligible for Scotland who wanted him in their set-up. Was Scotland Premier League Young Player of the Year in 2008-09 during is time at Hamilton.

FABIAN DELPH *Aston Villa*

POSITION: MIDFIELDER
DATE OF BIRTH: NOVEMBER 21, 1989
PLACE OF BIRTH: BRADFORD, WEST YORKSHIRE
INTERNATIONAL: ENGLAND UNDER-19 AND 21.

Although he hasn't made as many appearances for Villa as he might have expected since his £6m move from Leeds in summer 2009, Delph is still very highly rated. Villans manager Martin O'Neill is carefully supervising the youngster's development in a squad that is highly charged with young England stars and expects him to make as big an impact as James Milner, Gabby Agbonlahor and Ashley Young in the very near future. The 2009 Football League Young Player of the Year. A knee injury also curtailed his progress at the end of the 2009-10 season.

WOJCIECH SZCZESNY *Arsenal*

POSITION: KEEPER
DATE OF BIRTH: APRIL 18, 1990
PLACE OF BIRTH: WARSAW, POLAND
INTERNATIONAL: POLAND UNDER-21

He broke both arms in the gym just over a year ago, but the young Pole could soon be leaping up the ranks at The Emirates. Currently fourth choice, he is highly rated by boss Arsene Wenger who gave him a run out in the Carling Cup game against West Brom. He made his debut for Legia Warsaw at the age of just 15!

15

ONES TO WATCH: SPECIAL REPORT
UNITED DREAM TEAM

TOM CLEVERLEY

was just 11 when Sir Alex Ferguson invited him to join Manchester United.

"I was only a young lad and the facilities I saw were mind blowing, a totally different word from training on a night at Bradford City," admitted Tom.

His first stop was United's Carrington training ground before heading for a look at Old Trafford where he was lost for words when he stood on the pitch.

He admits: "When I first went there I was a bit star struck - you see the likes of Beckham and Giggs but you have to learn to live with it, let it be natural and grow up.

"I don't think anyone would be able to turn down the chance to play for one of the biggest clubs in the world and I am no different.

"True, anywhere else would have to be regarded as down but you only have to look at the likes of Ryan Shawcross [Stoke] and Frazier Campbell [Sunderland] who have gone on to make fantastic Premiership careers after leaving United. And Gerard Pique - he went on to win the Champions League and play in the World Cup."

With successful loan spells at Leicester and Watford - where he was the 2009-10 Player of the Season - behind him, Tom is now aiming to make a name for himself at United.

But now he's no longer awestruck: "I have seen the players when I have reported back to Carrington and when they played Arsenal at The Emirates last season I was there with the squad and had pre-match with them.

"I know Warren Joyce, the reserve team manager, watched a lot of my games for Watford and United got a monthly report of how I was doing. He's been great with me and I am sure that the specialist coaching from Ole Gunnar Solskjaer helped too," said Tom who hit 11 goals in 33 Championship games for Watford.

Ambitions

Most professional footballers would play anywhere to get the chance to help their side – although they like to specialise in one position. Tom is no different.

"I grew up playing as a full-back for the youth team but have now moved into midfield. I have played on the left, the right and in the centre.

"I will just say I am a versatile midfielder! I wouldn't say I have a specialist position but prefer left or centre," admits the 20-year-old who would love to follow in the footsteps of David Beckham and Ji-Sung Park.

And then there is playing for England Under-21s: "There is nothing better – apart from scoring at the Stretford End – they both come close to each other!

"When you pull on that shirt, they play the national anthem and you are lined up with quality players it is just what I have dreamt about since I was young."

What it's like to play for one of the biggest clubs in the world!

Bonus!

As he was only a boy, there was no transfer fee when Tom joined Man United – but the Premier League side agreed to pay their smaller relations compensation.

"I don't know exact figures but if Bradford City can benefit from my progress I would be delighted," said Tom, a former season ticket holder with the Yorkshire side.

"I still have a soft spot for them, still support them and want to see them do well."

Gaffer Tapes

It's boss talk, manager speak, a game of two halves - we all love a few words from the gaffer!

Wife worry

"She's got no chance of watching us next season. She hasn't got a clue about football but watches on the telly if it's on."

Superstitious Spurs boss Harry Redknapp tells missus Sandra to stay at home after she went to see his side lose their FA Cup semi-final at Wembley!

Tangerine talk

"We're not some useless load of Muppets who won't get ten points. Hopefully we won't be last on Match of the Day."

Ian Holloway hopes his promoted Blackpool won't make a Miss Piggy of things...

How tickled was he?

"I don't subscribe to the view that they turn up here and we roll over on our bellies, get tickled and say thanks for that."

Wolves boss Mick McCarthy then saw Arsenal trounce his side 4-1!

Hail Caesar

"In England it rains every day but still people sometimes tell me it is a beautiful day. That's when I tell them about Julius Caesar, who spent so much time in Britain yet, in the end, opted to move back to Italy."

Carlo Ancelotti's boss at Chelsea is also a Roman but Blues fans hope he is not leaving for Russia!

Target man

"It's sod's law it would be him that scored as we tried to sign him. I'll wring his neck, or try to."

Steve Bruce wasn't happy when Adam Johnson scored a wonder-strike equaliser for new club Man City.

Goal shock

"I couldn't believe that Salif Diao scored. He struggles to get beyond the half-way line, let alone getting into the box."

Stoke boss Tony Pulis checks for nose bleeds after a surprise goal.

Replacing the irreplaceable

"You can talk about the successful managers right now who might be on everyone's list. But in two years, they may not be. Or even next year. So it's very difficult to say who would replace me when my time came."

Sir Alex Ferguson ponders his successor at Man United. He'd be on anyone list, any year!

SPAIN REIGN!

Spain became the first team in football history to win the World Cup after losing their opening game – and only the third to be both World and European champions.

A dramatic goal from Andres Iniesta just four minutes from the end of extra-time clinched their 1-0 victory against Holland.

A swift Spanish counter-attack caught ten-man Holland cold, with Iniesta rifling home the winner after a clever pass from Cesc Fabregas.

It was no less than Spain deserved. Defeat to Switzerland in their first group match led some fans to question the pre-tournament favourites, but they stuck to their footballing ideals and bounced back to win the biggest football competition of them all.

A tale of two teams

Barcelona and Real Madrid, Spain's two biggest clubs, provided the bulk of the players for their country's World Cup victory.

Barcelona contributed a remarkable SEVEN of Spain's starting eleven in the final, plus reserve keeper Victor Valdes. Two Barca old boys, youth graduates Pepe Reina and Cesc Fabregas, were also in the 23-man squad.

Real saw three of their players start the final, with two more – Raul Abiol and Alvaro Arbeloa – in the squad. Juan Manuel Mata, now of Valencia, came through the youth ranks at the Bernabeu too.

Barca's boys...

Gerard Pique: Started his career at Barca, before a four-year spell with Man United. A mainstay of the Catalans' all conquering line-up.

Carles Puyol: Alongside Pique for club and country is Puyol, another Barca graduate.

Andres Iniesta: The match-winner has earned rave reviews for Barcelona in recent seasons.

Xavi: Another Barca partnership, Xavi and Iniesta's bond is almost telepathic.

Sergio Busquets: The young midfielder only established himself at Barcelona over the last two seasons, but is now a first choice.

David Villa: Completed a move to Barcelona on the eve of the World Cup. One of the most prolific strikers around.

Pedro: On the back of his first season in the Barcelona first-team, Pedro started a World Cup Final!

From the first whistle of the final they were champions, as the Netherlands' game plan consisted solely of stopping Spain play football, rather than concentrate on their own game.

English Premier League referee Howard Webb must have hoped for an easier evening. He had to dish out a record 13 yellow cards, including the sending-off of John Heitinga for a second booking in extra-time.

And the rest!

Just ten of Spain's 23-man squad weren't with Barcelona or Real Madrid on the day of the final...

Pepe Reina: Liverpool stopper, started his career at Barca before leaving to pursue first-team football.

Carlos Marchena: Valencia defender made three substitute appearances during the tournament.

Cesc Fabregas: Signed by Arsenal from Barca's youth academy.

Javi Martinez: Athletic Bilbao playmaker made one sub appearance.

David Silva: Manchester City winger started his career with Valencia. Started the first game then made one substitute appearance.

Jesus Navas: Sevilla man had just one start.

Fernando Torres: Liverpool star was eventually dropped for the semi-final and final.

Juan Manuel Mata: Valencia winger started at Real Madrid.

Fernando Llorente: Bilbao forward made one sub appearance.

Madrid's men...

Iker Casillas: World Cup victory will surely cement his role as one of the greatest keepers of all time. National team captain.

Sergio Ramos: Possibly the best right-back in the world, Ramos's marauding runs have been a trademark for Spain.

Xabi Alonso: Alonso bounced back from a trophy-less debut campaign with Real to lift international honours.

THE CAPTAINS

STEVEN GERRARD (left) became the tenth player to captain England at World Cup finals when he led them out at South Africa 2010. Three of those players - Terry Butcher, Mick Mills and Peter Shilton - took the armband when the real skipper was unable to do his job. Here are the nine leaders...

BILLY WRIGHT 1950, 1954, 1958

The Wolves defender played 105 games for England between 1946 and 1959. The 1952 Football Writers' Footballer of the Year has a stand named after him at Molineux where he is still a legend.

JOHNNY HAYNES 1962

The first player to earn £100 a week, Haynes was an exceptionally gifted player who turned out a club record 658 times for Fulham. Another player with a stand named after him, and like Wright also has a statue outside of Craven Cottage.

BOBBY MOORE 1966, 1970

Will forever be remembered as the cultured West Ham defender who lifted the World Cup for England on home soil. His statue is outside the new Wembley, a fitting tribute to a man who sadly died of cancer at the age of just 51 in 1993.

MICK MILLS 1982

The Ipswich full-back was a Mr Dependable for both Ipswich and England and was handed the captain's armband for the games when the Three Lions lost Kevin Keegan to injury during Spain 1982.

BRYAN ROBSON 1986, 1990

Manchester United and England's battling Captain Marvel was injured in the second World Cup game of 1986 and Shilton took over. In 1990, he also suffered a series of injuries during the group stages.

PETER SHILTON
1986, 1990

England's record cap holder with 125 international appearances, the keeper who made his name with Leicester and Forest kept a record ten clean sheets in World Cup finals. He didn't even make his finals debut until the age of 32. The man who was victim to Maradona's "Hand of God" goal.

TERRY BUTCHER 1990

When Robson was injured at Italia 90, Butcher stepped into the breach. He had made his name as a skilled defender at Ipswich and Rangers and will forever be remembered for playing with his head bloodied and bandaged after being injured during a qualifier for those finals.

ALAN SHEARER 1998

Appointed captain for the 1998 World Cup qualifiers, goal-king Shearer, the Premier League's top scorer of all-time, played 63 times for his country, scoring 30 goals. Retired from international football after Euro 2000.

DAVID BECKHAM
2002, 2006

England's most-capped outfield player with 115 appearances, tearfully announced he was standing down as skipper after the 2006 World Cup. He was then dropped – but was pulled out of the international wilderness by Fabio Capello and would have played a part at South Africa 2010 had it not been for injury.

Best Celebration

Siphiwe Tshabalala
(South Africa v Mexico)

After his thunderous effort to mark the first goal of the tournament, Tshabalala sprinted to the opposite sideline to perform a choreographed dance routine with four of his team-mates. The whole of South Africa erupted to Tshabalala's goal.

Biggest Controversy
England's goal that never was...

It's a moment we'll never forget. After an awful first half hour against the Germans, England were suddenly back in with a shout of winning the knockout round tie. Matthew Upson halved the deficit to 2-1 and then a superb lob from Frank Lampard levelled up matters. But the 'goal' was not given (despite the ball being some distance over the line). Germany went on to add two more goals.

Shoot World

The good, the bad and the crazy from South Africa 2010

Biggest Howler
Rob Green (England v USA)

Robert Green has had to endure his fair share of criticism for his horrific misjudgement against America, but its significance doesn't pale – if he hadn't let the goal in, England would've topped the group and avoided a battering by Germany. The path to the semis would've been fairly comfortable, even for an out of sorts side like Fabio Capello's. To be fair to Green, he wasn't the only keeper that struggled with the much-criticised ball.

Move of the Tournament
Germany's fourth in the 4-1 win over England

Defending an England free-kick, Germany killed off the game with a stunning counter-attack. Thomas Muller got the ball in his own half and picked out Bastian Schweinsteiger on the left flank. Schweinsteiger powered forward, cutting in and returned to Muller to winner.

Cup Awards

Best Simulation
Fernando Torres (Spain v Chile)

The Liverpool forward was, once again, lacklustre. But his impact on Spain's group stage victory over Chile cannot be denied. His pressing forced David Villa's long-range opener and his outrageous first-half dive ensured that his opponents were reduced to ten men. In the move that ultimately led to Spain's second goal, Torres went down like he had been shot despite no contact – and Marco Estrada was given his marching orders as a result.

Save of the Tournament
Luis Suarez (Uruguay v Ghana)

The Ajax frontman came into the World Cup as the hottest forward in Europe – having notched an incredible 49 goals the previous season – but he will be best remembered for a save! Suarez single-handedly – literally – saved Uruguay from a quarter-final knockout by palming away Dominic Adiyiah's goal-bound effort in the final minute of extra-time, having already denied Stephen Appiah's header with his knee. Ghana missed the subsequent penalty and Uruguay won the penalty shoot-out.

Unluckiest man of the Tournament
Asamoah Gyan (Ghana)

Gyan was the catalyst for Ghana's remarkable progression to the quarter-finals, grabbing three crucial goals. As he stepped up to take a penalty in the last minute of extra-time against Uruguay, it seemed Gyan was destined for mega-stardom. Converting the penalty would mean that Ghana were the first African team to reach the World Cup semi-finals and that he'd equal Roger Milla's African record of four World Cup goals in a single tournament. His effort was blazed against the bar and Ghana were knocked out on penalties.

Worst Haircut
Gervinho (Ivory Coast)

You have to give him credit, Gervinho's approach to premature hair loss is admirable and unique. Despite his hairline receding dramatically, Gervinho persisted with his dreadlock-esque style, putting a headband across his forehead to try and diminish its appearance. Sorry, but it doesn't work...

Goal of the Tournament
Giovanni van Bronckhorst (Holland v Uruguay)

The Dutch captain, playing his last before retirement, set his side on their way to victory with an absolute corker. Found on the left flank, van Bronckhorst, with what looked to be a hopeful effort, strike found the top corner of the net off the far post, brilliantly

STAT ATTACK!

Facts and figures from World Cup 2010

Player of the Tournament
Diego Forlan
(Uruguay)

Best young player
Thomas Muller
(Germany), age 20

Team with most goals
Germany 16

Golden Boot
Thomas Muller
(Germany)
* He scored five goals, along with Diego Forlan (Uruguay), Wesley Sneijder (Holland) and David Villa (Spain) but got the award using minutes played and assists as a tie-breaker.

Most shots 33
Asamoah Gyan
(Ghana)

IN NUMBERS

62 games

145 goals

3 billion watched the tournament on television

Most saves
Richard Kingson
(Ghana) 24

First goal
Siphiwe Tshabalala for hosts South Africa
55 minutes into the first game of the tournament, against Mexico.

Biggest win
Portugal 7 North Korea 0

Teams with least goals
Algeria and Honduras 0

First red card
Nicolas Lodeiro, Uruguay
81 minutes into his side's 0-0 draw with France on day one. He had come on as a second-half sub and got two yellow cards.

INTERESTING FACTS

- With four goals in three consecutive World Cup games – thanks to his strike in the last 16 – David Villa equalled a Spanish record first set by Zarra in 1950.

- Japan kicked off all four of their games with the same starting line-up.

- Seven of the eight Round of 16 matches were won by group winners. The exception was Group D runners-up Ghana who beat the USA.

- Puyol, Pique, Busquets, Xavi, Iniesta, Pedro and Villa ensured Spain become only the third team to start a World Cup semi-final with seven players from the same club – Barcelona.

- Spain became only the third team hold the European Championship and World Cup at the same time. Italy went into the finals as Euro champs in 1970 and Germany in 1974. France won the World Cup in 1998 and the Euros two years later.

- Germany may have been knocked out in the semis, but that was their 100th World Cup finals game. They are now ahead of Brazil (99 games) Italy (80) Argentina (70) and England (59).

- Policeman Howard Webb, 38, from Rotherham, South Yorkshire, became the first Englishman to referee the World Cup Final since Jack Taylor in 1974.

- Holland's John Heitinga became the fifth player to be sent off in a World Cup Final, thanks to his two yellows in the game against Spain.

259 yellow and red cards

72 year-old Greek boss Otto Rehhagel became the oldest coach in World Cup finals history

18 year-old Christian Eriksen (Denmark) was the youngest player

27

TEN WORLD CUP 2010
MEMORIES....

SOUTH AFRICA SCORING

With 55 minutes on the clock it was fitting that the first goal of the tournament should go to the home nation as South Africa's Siphiwe Tshabalala put them ahead against Mexico. Raphael Marquez's equaliser meant it wasn't to be a perfect start, but at least we'd had a pretty quick tear-jerking highlight.

VUVUZELAS

Will the world ever be quite the same? Or should that be quiet the same? The noisy plastic Vuvuzela horns deafened players and fans and even led to tennis bosses at Wimbledon banning them! England's Jamie Carragher still can't escape them as his children asked for two to be brought back from Africa!

MAICON'S MAGIC GOAL

How did Brazil's raiding right-back get the ball into the net from such an acute angle against North Korea? The Inter Milan defender was almost on the line when he somehow managed to get the ball to curl into the net. He claims it was an attempt – and you can't doubt him as he scored a similar one against Portugal two years ago!

SWISS BEATING SPAIN

Everyone loves an underdog, so to see the admirable Swiss make Spain squirm brought a smile to many a neutral face. Spain played well enough but they lacked the killer instinct that joint tournament favourites should have had in a game like this. Gelson Fernandes's goal came after some sheer determination against the champions-to-be.

FIRST SENDING OFF

It didn't take long – the second game and the first sending off as Uruguay's Nicolas Lodeiro got his marching orders against France. The sub had only been on the pitch for 16 minutes when he got his second yellow but of course the unpredictable French couldn't cash in and we got a bore draw. France would head home after failure at the first hurdle.

G MEN...

Stevie G didn't keep us waiting long for England's first goal – just four minutes – but before the end of the very disappointing 1-1 draw with the USA we'd also had another moment to forget... Rob Green's goal-keeping howler. Green's goof meant a number of fans forgot to mention Emile Heskey's

NORTH KOREA FRIGHTEN BRAZIL

The five-times World Champions and tournament joint-favourites against the minnows of the competition and ranked 105th in the world. But no one appeared to have told North Korea they weren't meant to worry Brazil! Korea striker Jong Tae-se cried during their National Anthem, his side went 2-0 down but then Yun-Nam Ji had the audacity to score a minute from time and leave fans wondering if an unlikely draw was possible. It wasn't... final score 2-1!

FOOTBALLER COMING HOME

We English never learn! Hyped up as possible World Champions, the Three Lions whimpered through the three opening games. A 1-0 victory against Slovenia was hardly stunning. And wouldn't you just know it – the Germans awaited us. Extra-time and penalties? Oh how we wish that's what had happened! That could have been regarded as a facesaver – instead a 4-1 crushing at the hands of the old rivals was a very bitter pill to swallow.

SEVEN HEAVEN FOR PORTUGAL

Bore draws and a lack of goals meant it wasn't the greatest start to the World Cup. But when Portugal found their feet it was the hapless North Koreans who were put to the sword. Cristiano Ronaldo's men smashed them 7-0 with a glittering display of football – which probably wasn't screened to the Koreans back home due to censorship involving much of the action in the tournament.

GOOD ON YOU GHANA

Robbed by injury of one of their best players – Chelsea's Michael Essien – Ghana proved they are not just a one-man team. The Black Stars became the first and only African nation to qualify for the quarter-finals on home soil thanks to their 2-1 win against the USA in the Round of 16. Ghana are only the third African side to reach this stage, following Senegal and Cameroon.

SPOT THE BOSS

THERE'S A YOUNG PLAYER MAKING A BIG NAME FOR HIMSELF AND A HOST OF PREMIER LEAGUE MANAGERS ARE ON A SCOUTING MISSION.

They didn't want to be spotted by club officials so they bought a ticket like anyone else and tried to disappear into the crowd. Can you find them hidden among the fans? Answers page 110

We know six managers are at the game, so we want you to find:

- Sir Alex Ferguson
- David Moyes
- Sam Allardyce
- Harry Redknapp
- Arsene Wenger
- Steve Bruce

10

1. Park began his career with Kyoto Purple Sanga in Japan's second division but really made a name for himself at PSV Eindhoven who were persuaded to sell him to Manchester United in 2005 for £4m.

2. When Park first arrived at Old Trafford many supporters believed the player had only been bought so that the club could cash in by selling shirts bearing his name to fans in the Far East. They have been proved wrong!

3. United fans sing a song joking about Park eating your pet dog - which he obviously doesn't do! But when he was growing up he admits that his father got him to drink FROG juice to help him grow!

4. PSV fans also sang a song about Park when he was with them in Holland and included it on an official club CD. It just repeated his name - in Dutch - over and over again.

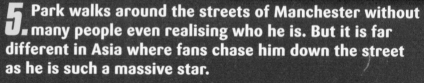

5. Park walks around the streets of Manchester without many people even realising who he is. But it is far different in Asia where fans chase him down the street as he is such a massive star.

6. The young player who was rejected by his college teams played in the World Cup semi-finals for South Korea in 2002.

7. His nickname is "Three-lung Park" because he just never stops running from one end of the pitch to the other, ensuring he is never far from the thick of the action.

8. Park has three Premier League winner's medals. He was also the first Asian player to appear in a Champions League Final, the defeat to Barcelona in 2009.

9. He is only the eighth South Korea captain to take his country's side to the World Cup finals. Only two of them have more caps that he has won so far.

10. He has a deal with Manchester United until 2012 and is thought to earn around £65,000 a week. Park has said he never wants to leave 'the best club in the world'.

IT'S A FACT...

Name:
Park Ji-Sung

Birth Date:
February 25, 1981

Birth Place:
Seoul, South Korea

Position:
Midfielder

Clubs:
Kyoto Purple Sanga,
PSV Eindhoven,
Manchester United.

35

FAVOURITE PLAYERS

You know the players you love to watch and admire. But who do Premier League stars look up to? We asked a few of them...

THEO WALCOTT

NOMINATED BY:
MANUEL ALMUNIA, ARSENAL

"He is by far the most exciting English player I have ever seen. His skills are incredible and I am sure that over 100 metres he would get a good time. With the ball he is also good technically."

RUUD VAN NISTELROOY

NOMINATED BY:
BOBBY ZAMORA, FULHAM

"His game is all about what I have tried to do. Stay up there in and around the box, hold things up, set people up and just get shots off. He is pretty much the master at that sort of football."

FERNANDO TORRES

NOMINATED BY:
DARREN BENT, SUNDERLAND

"He is one of the best strikers in the world. He's brilliant and when he is playing at his best he is unstoppable. If I can be up there with him in the scoring charts I will be delighted."

JAMES MILNER

NOMINATED BY:
JOHN CAREW, ASTON VILLA

"He is strong mentally and has been amazing for our team. James has a great football head as well as the skills. He still chases the ball to the corner flag in the final minute when most people's legs have gone, he is amazing."

STEVEN GERRARD

NOMINATED BY:
DAN AGGER, LIVERPOOL

"He is not only a brilliant footballer, he is also a really good person, a strong character who helps others. Stevie would fit into any team in the world. He is a fantastic captain and every player in the team will say he has helped them in one way or another."

RYAN GIGGS

NOMINATED BY:
PHIL NEVILLE, EVERTON

"He is my hero. I think he is the greatest player ever to play for Man United. I know United have had some great players but he's won everything, he's broken almost every record, so he stands alone now as probably one of the greatest players who has ever lived."

KNOW YOUR FOOTBALL

TRANSFER TRACKER

IT'S EASY TO TELL US WHICH TEAMS THE FOLLOWING PLAYERS WERE WITH AT THE END OF THE 2009-10 SEASON. BUT WE WANT YOU TO TELL US THE SIDE THEY PLAYED FOR <u>BEFORE</u> THEY JOINED THAT TEAM – AND LOANS DON'T COUNT.

PLAYER	2009-10	PREVIOUSLY
Peter Crouch	Tottenham	Liverpool
Danny Guthrie	Newcastle	
Maxi Rodriguez	Liverpool	
Carlos Tevez	Man City	Man United
Yuri Zhirkov	Chelsea	
Gabriel Obertan	Man United	

GROUND ZERO

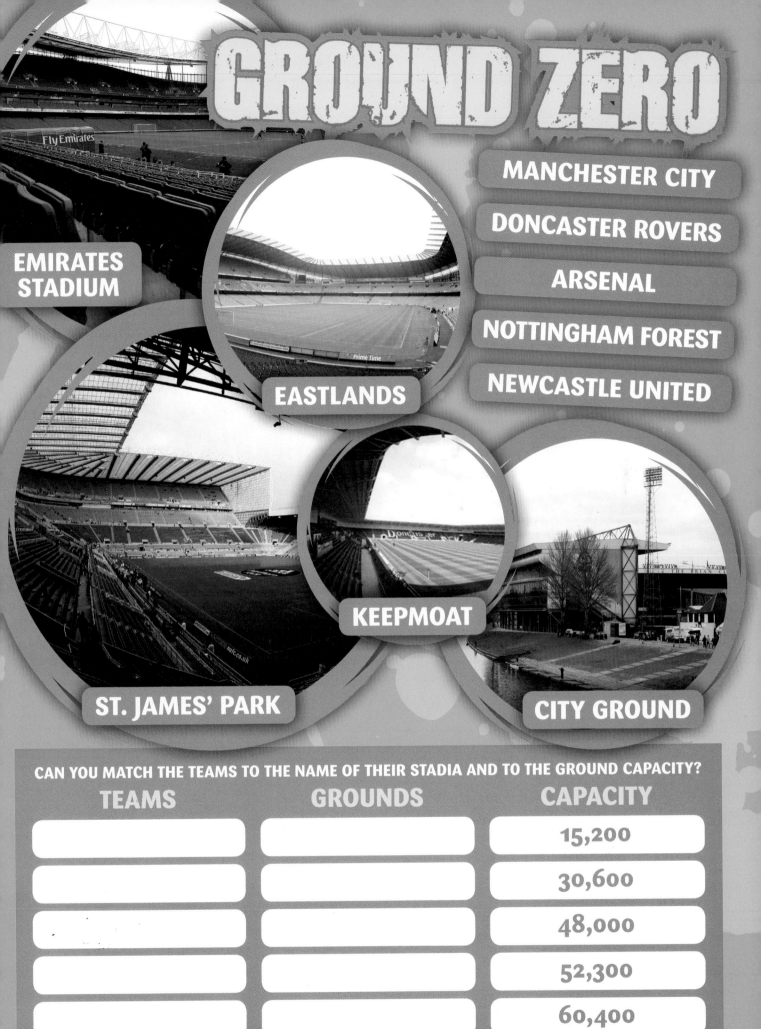

EMIRATES STADIUM

EASTLANDS

KEEPMOAT

ST. JAMES' PARK

CITY GROUND

MANCHESTER CITY

DONCASTER ROVERS

ARSENAL

NOTTINGHAM FOREST

NEWCASTLE UNITED

CAN YOU MATCH THE TEAMS TO THE NAME OF THEIR STADIA AND TO THE GROUND CAPACITY?

TEAMS	GROUNDS	CAPACITY
		15,200
		30,600
		48,000
		52,300
		60,400

YOU WHAT?

SOME GOOD, BAD, UGLY AND DOWNRIGHT SILLY QUOTES FROM THE SOMETIMES STRANGE WORLD OF FOOTBALL

BOXING CLEVER

"I couldn't believe that Salif Diao scored. He struggles to get beyond the half way line, let alone getting into the box."

Stoke boss Tony Pulis checks for nose bleeds after a surprise goal.

HOT WHEELS

"One letter asked if they could have my car. You do get some pretty bizarre requests."

Fan mail took on a new meaning for England keeper Joe Hart.

HIM WE LIKE

"He's like Yoda. His pearls of wisdom seem to be far-reaching and he speaks a lot of sense."

Keeper David James reckons Avram Grant had the Force as Pompey boss.

STREET-WISE

"I do like it. I don't understand some things but it seems very good."

Carlos Tevez admits he is hooked on... Coronation Street!

COMPLIMENTS OF THE SEASON

WHO WON WHAT IN 2009-2010

CHAMPIONSHIP CHAMPIONS

NEWCASTLE UNITED

AUTOMATIC PROMOTION:	PLAY-OFF FINAL:
WEST BROMWICH ALBION	BLACKPOOL 3 CARDIFF CITY 2

LEAGUE ONE CHAMPIONS

NORWICH CITY

AUTOMATIC PROMOTION:	PLAY-OFF FINAL:
LEEDS UNITED	MILLWALL 1 SWINDON 0

LEAGUE TWO CHAMPIONS

NOTTS COUNTY

AUTOMATIC PROMOTION:	PLAY-OFF FINAL:
ROCHDALE BOURNEMOUTH	DAGENHAM 3 ROTHERHAM 2

SCOTTISH PREMIER LEAGUE

RANGERS

Gers notched their 53rd title to increase their own world record. They were eight points clear of their nearest rivals Celtic – even though they did lose the final Old Firm game of the season 2-1 at Celtic Park.

SCOTTISH CUP

DUNDEE UNITED

First Division Ross County kept it goal-less for the first-half before the Tangerines secured a 3-0 win thanks to David Goodwille and two late strikes from Craig Conway. It was United's second-ever Scottish Cup win.

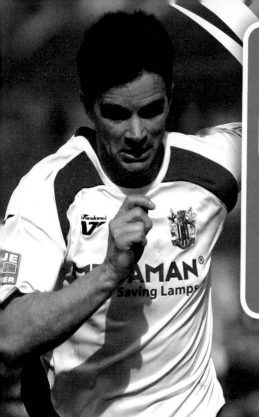

BLUE SQUARE PREMIER CHAMPIONS

STEVENAGE BOROUGH

Boro clinched the title with two games to spare and get their place in the Football League 14 years late! When they won the Conference in 1996 they were denied promotion as their ground didn't meet league standards.

PLAY-OFF FINAL: OXFORD UNITED 3   YORK CITY 1

FA CUP

CHELSEA

Two missed penalties, the woodwork rattled five times by the winners in the first-half and a missed sitter. The clash between Portsmouth and Chelsea wasn't dull – and you could have guessed in advance that the only goal would be scored by Didier Drogba, his seventh cup final goal for the Blues.

CIS CUP

RANGERS

Gers had two players sent-off but managed to win the CIS Cup 1-0 against St. Mirren thanks to a Kenny Miller goal seven minutes from time.

LEAGUE CUP

MANCHESTER UNITED

James Milner gave Aston Villa a fourth minute lead with a penalty but it wasn't long before United clicked into gear. Michael Owen brought them level after 12 minutes but then had to depart with an injury. That allowed Wayne Rooney to take to the pitch having surprisingly being left on the bench – and he headed the winner in the 73rd minute.

EURO STARS

The teams who conquered Europe's major leagues last season.

FRANCE
CHAMPIONS: MARSEILLE
RUNNERS-UP: LYON

ITALY
CHAMPIONS: INTER MILAN
RUNNERS-UP: ROMA

CHAMPIONS LEAGUE	THE FA TROPHY
BAYERN MUNICH 0	BARROW 2
INTER MILAN 2	STEVENAGE BOROUGH 1
EUROPA LEAGUE	THE FA VASE
ATLETICO MADRID 2	WHITLEY BAY 6
FULHAM 0	WROXHAM 1

JOHNSTONE'S PAINTS TROPHY

SOUTHAMPTON

Saints demolished Carlisle 4-1 with goals from Ricky Lambert, Adam Lallana, Papa Waigo and Antonio. Gary Madine got a consolation near the end in front of a 73,000 crowd at Wembley.

PFA YOUNG PLAYER OF THE YEAR

JAMES MILNER

It doesn't matter where he plays on the pitch, the Leeds-born England man always works his socks off. Left, right, centre, defence, striker - you can play him anywhere and he will have an impact. His crosses are often second to none.

PFA AND FOOTBALL WRITERS' PLAYER OF THE YEAR

WAYNE ROONEY

Who's Cristiano Ronaldo? There was doom and gloom at Old Trafford when the Portugeeser left - Roonster stepped up to the plate and showed there was no need for worry. A glut of goals - 34 in total - and his usual non-stop battling performances raised his game to new, higher levels than even the fans expected.

SPAIN	GERMANY	HOLLAND
CHAMPIONS: BARCELONA	CHAMPIONS: BAYERN MUNICH	CHAMPIONS: FC TWENTE
RUNNERS-UP: REAL MADRID	RUNNERS-UP: SCHALKE 04	RUNNERS-UP: AJAX

WHO NEEDS FRIENDS?

Manchester City and England defender **Joleon Lescott** has been kicked into touch - by his own son!

Little Donovan Lescott has City and Barcelona shirts but his pride and joy is a Manchester United kit because he thinks Wayne Rooney is the business.

Lescott wasn't the only one with people problems... his City boss **Roberto Mancini** popped into his local church for a service and got a bit of a shock.

The religious gaffer didn't know that the priest at St. John's Roman Catholic Church was a Manchester United fan!

TOP TRIVIA

Amazing, stupid, silly and serious stuff about top footballers - including things they may not want you to know!

JT ON TV

John Terry can't get enough of football on telly - he even watches non-league games. The only time he hands over the remote to wife Toni is when they both watch the X Factor and Only Fools and Horses.

We just hope he doesn't go through the same ritual at home as he does before every home game.

Then, the Chelsea and England skipper has to use the same toilet cubicle at Stamford Bridge before every match, even if he has to queue and wait his turn.

STINGER!

Italy defender **Fabio Cannavaro** was floored by a bee!

The 2006 World Cup-winner was stung by the insect and had to have a cortisone injection.

But that meant he tested positive when he was given a routine drugs test, and almost led to him being banned from the game!

WOULD YOU BELIEVE IT...

⚽ Football players on council-run pitches were told they couldn't play extra-time as their bookings were for just one game of 90 minutes plus half-time! If the players at **Haltwhistle** in Northumberland wanted more time they had to apply months in advance to the council!

⚽ **Cristiano Ronaldo** is believed to do 3,000 sit ups a day to keep in trim – whilst he watches the telly. Meanwhile, Ronnie is collecting valuable watches as he realises they can increase in value over time.

⚽ Wolves defender **Jody Craddock** paints pictures, often of big name stars like John Terry.

⚽ Millwall defender **Darren Ward**, who runs a cattery in Hertfordshire with his wife Sam, reckons: "They eat like Royalty, better than I do!"

⚽ Aston Villa boss **Martin O'Neill** admits to liking rock groups The Killers, Kasabian, Snow Patrol and Oasis thanks to his daughters. But he also likes Bob Dylan, the Small Faces and The Who.

⚽ Defender **Gary Neville** had trees planted near his home that spelt out the initials of his beloved Manchester United!

⚽ A giant screen in the **Man United** changing room tells their stars all of their appointments they have to keep, including haircuts, massage and who has to run the bath!

⚽ An **Ipswich Town** fan who had been unconscious for three weeks after a fall came out of his coma when his mother played a commentary of his team's game to him.

CAR WARS

Manchester City midfielder **Stephen Ireland** dropped a big clanger when he forked out tens of thousands of pounds for a sports Audi - with trims in red, the colour of rivals United!

He had to cough up another £10,000 to get the red bits changed to blue, including the petrol cap and the number seven on the wheel trims - the same numeral as his shirt number.

Meanwhile, France defender **William Gallas** is thought to have forked out £350,000 to buy a chrome plated Mercedes Benz SLR McLaren. It's got a top speed of more than 200mph!

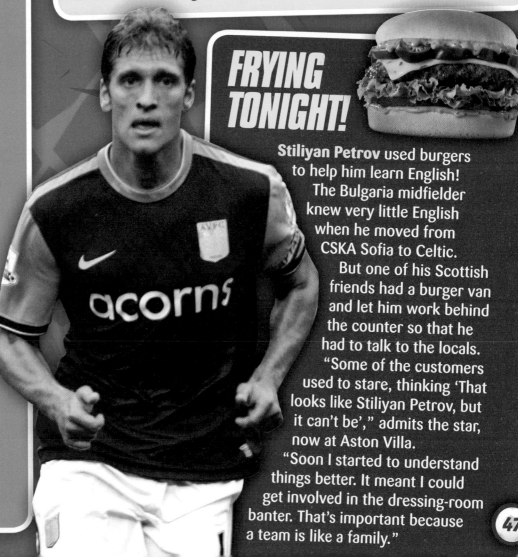

FRYING TONIGHT!

Stiliyan Petrov used burgers to help him learn English! The Bulgaria midfielder knew very little English when he moved from CSKA Sofia to Celtic.

But one of his Scottish friends had a burger van and let him work behind the counter so that he had to talk to the locals.

"Some of the customers used to stare, thinking 'That looks like Stiliyan Petrov, but it can't be'," admits the star, now at Aston Villa.

"Soon I started to understand things better. It meant I could get involved in the dressing-room banter. That's important because a team is like a family."

A-Z QUIZ

TEST YOUR KNOWLEDGE OF TOP PLAYERS WHO HAVE OR DO APPEAR IN THE PREMIER LEAGUE! THE ALPHABET WILL GIVE YOU CLUES TO THEIR NAMES...

B Jimmy who has played for Wigan, Fulham and Hull City.

Bollard

C Three England stars are Coles. We want the striker...

ENGLAND

Andy

A Arsenal's Russian striker bought from Zenit St. Petersburg.

Andrey Arshavin

D Scores on the Daws for this former Nottingham Forest defender now earning his Spurs.

Dawson

E Striker with Croatian and Brazilian connections who used to play for Dinamo Zagreb.

F
Veteran keeper who left Rovers to become a Villan.

Friedel

G
The £10m Scotland keeper who used to play for Hearts.

McGregor

H
His name sounds Spanish but Chelsea's No.2 keeper is Portuguese.

I
No relation to Ozzy, this midfielder has had loans with Forest and Boro.

J
Argentina World Cup winger who has suffered relegation and promotion in the Premier League.

Jonas Gutierrez

K
Ivory Coast forward with Chelsea - and it's not Drogba!

L
Midfielder who helped Sunderland to promotion then became a Potter.

N

One brother is at Man United, the other at Everton. We want their surname.

neville

M

Scotland striker at St. Andrews.

O

Nigerian-born defender has played for England Under-21s.

Q

Former Boro and Birmingham City defender.

R

Midfielder-defender and youngest-ever Everton player to appear in Europe.

rodwell

P

Premier League and England's tallest player.

peter crouch

S

Aussie star who upped sticks at Boro to join Fulham.

Schwarzer

18 78

Everton

NIL SATIS NISI OPTIMUM

U
Defender with Arsenal, Birmingham and West Ham.

T
This whirlwind striker is known as El Nino!

Torres

V
Dutch striker who left Celtic to become a Tiger.

Z
Argentina defender at Eastlands.

W
A hat-trick for England against Croatia in 2009

walcott

Y
Winger Ashley, a former Watford player, who became an England star.

young

X
Former Liverpool midfielder who went to Real Madrid.

Xabialonso

1. Crouchy began his career at Tottenham but was loaned out to non-league Dulwich Hamlet and Swedish side Hassleholm before a permanent move to QPR.

2. He has played for manager Harry Redknapp at three different clubs - Portsmouth, Southampton and Tottenham.

3. Three different England managers have called on Crouch's services - Sven Goran Eriksson, Steve McClaren and Fabio Capello.

4. At 6ft 7in Peter Crouch is the tallest player to turn out for England and was also the Premier League's tallest player until Austrian Stefan Maierhofer signed for Wolves in 2009 and Nikola Zigic for Wolves in 2010.

5. Portsmouth bought the player the first time for £1.25m, sold him to Villa for £5m, who sold him to Southampton for £5m before a £7m move to Liverpool. He rejoined Portsmouth for £11m before his £10m move to Spurs.

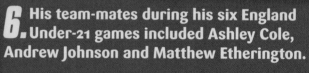

6. His team-mates during his six England Under-21 games included Ashley Cole, Andrew Johnson and Matthew Etherington.

7. Crouchy made his full England debut in May 2005 during a friendly against Colombia but it wasn't until the following March that he scored his first full international goal, in a win against Uruguay.

8. He scored a hat-trick in the 6-0 victory against Jamaica at Old Trafford during the warm-up to the 2006 World Cup finals - and missed a penalty during the same match.

9. His first tournament goal for England came at Germany 06 against Trinidad and Tobago. Crouchy scored 18 goals in his first 17 starts for the Three Lions.

10. Peter was voted the funniest man in British sport, netting 24% of the vote in a poll of 2,000 people.

TOTTENHAM HOTSPUR

WORLD CUP 2010 CHILE V SWITZERLAND

WORLD CUP 2010 ITALY V NEW ZEALAND

SPOT THE BALL

WORLD CUP 2010 SLOVENIA V ENGLAND

WORLD CUP 2010 USA V ALGERIA

You know how it works - we've removed the balls from these images taken at the World Cup finals of 2010 in South Africa. We've told you the teams the games involve and now we want you to use your footie knowledge to try and work out which grid references the ball was in.

Answers page 110.

PREMIER LEAGUE SECRETS

Inside information about your favourite stars – including stuff they may not even want you to know!

STAR TURN

Aaron Ramsey could have been playing with an oval ball instead of a round one.

The Wales midfielder played local rugby whilst he was at school and even had the chance to join Super League side St. Helens.

Luckily for his country and Arsenal fans the youngster – who was also a cross-country champion and 800 metre runner – decided football was his first love.

NASTY NIC?

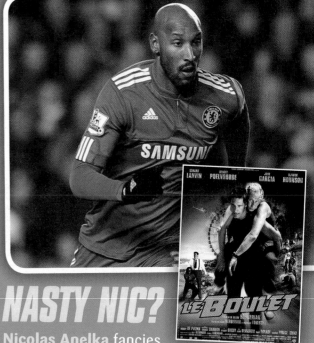

Nicolas Anelka fancies following in the footsteps of Vinnie Jones and Eric Cantona – and becoming an actor when he hangs up his boots.

The France and Chelsea striker has already had a part in a film called *Le Boulet*, which was produced by a friend, and admits he wants to play in all-action adventure films.

FROM THE HORSE'S MOUTH

You could say that striker **Sylvan Ebanks-Blake** has a bit of form – he was named after a racehorse! The former Man United striker was sold to Plymouth for £200,00 and then to Wolves for £1.5m. And not one to miss out on a decent bet, Old Trafford gaffer Sir Alex Ferguson said that if the player scored 100 goals in his first season he wanted to buy him back!

The player got his name because a friend of his father liked a bet and there was a horse called Sylvan's delight. He had a bet on the horse, won a few quid and at the time his son was on his way into the world!

WHEELY GOOD

Steven Gerrard is hot stuff on the pitch - but he's not so keen on hot wheels...

The Liverpool skipper sold his 190mph Aston Martin because he reckons it was a bit too quick for him and he's 'not the best driver in the world'.

Don't feel sorry for him though - he still has a collection of cars that include another Aston, Ferrari, Bentley, Porsche and Mercedes!

Meanwhile, the secret is out... Stevie G is a McFly fan! Mind you, believe that if you will, as Danny Murphy once tried to convince Shoot that his mate also owns Boyzone CDs!

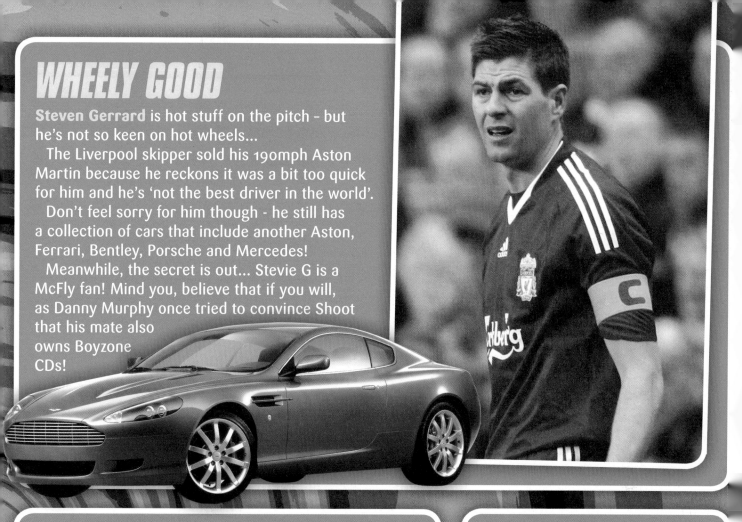

GETTING SHIRTY

Wales star **Craig Bellamy** admits that one of his biggest heroes is... team-mate Carlos Tevez.

The fiery striker even has the Argentina star's No.11 international shirt hanging in his home and has revealed he just loves watching his Man City colleague play.

"He knows all about the shirt and I might even get my little boy to get him to autograph it," admitted Bellars.

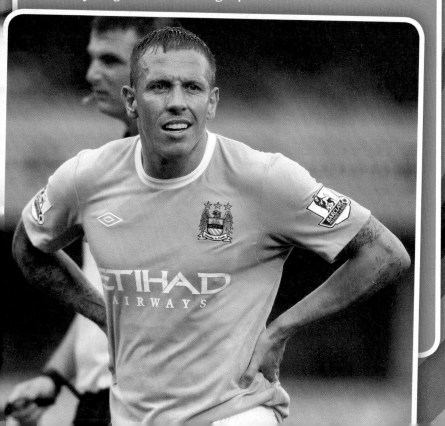

QUICK-KICKS

⚽ England and Man United defender **Gary Neville** has received an honorary degree from Bolton University.

⚽ **Carlos Tevez** wants to be on *Strictly Come Dancing* doing the tango. But the Argentina star reckons he is going to have to wait until he retires.

⚽ Bolton defender **Zat Knight** is followed wherever he goes by his family... even onto the pitch! The giant centre-half has his Grandad George's name tattooed on his right shoulder. On his left shoulder is a tattoo dedicated to son Kai.

⚽ Portsmouth midfielder **Michael Brown** reckons he can play until he's 40 thanks to a bit of a racket! He plays squash a few times every week against his mates because he believes it will boost his fitness levels and keep him sharp.

⚽ Midfield **Stephen Ireland** is up for a fight - a cage fight! The Republic of Ireland player has even had a crack at the sport with a grueling training regime that includes kick-boxing.

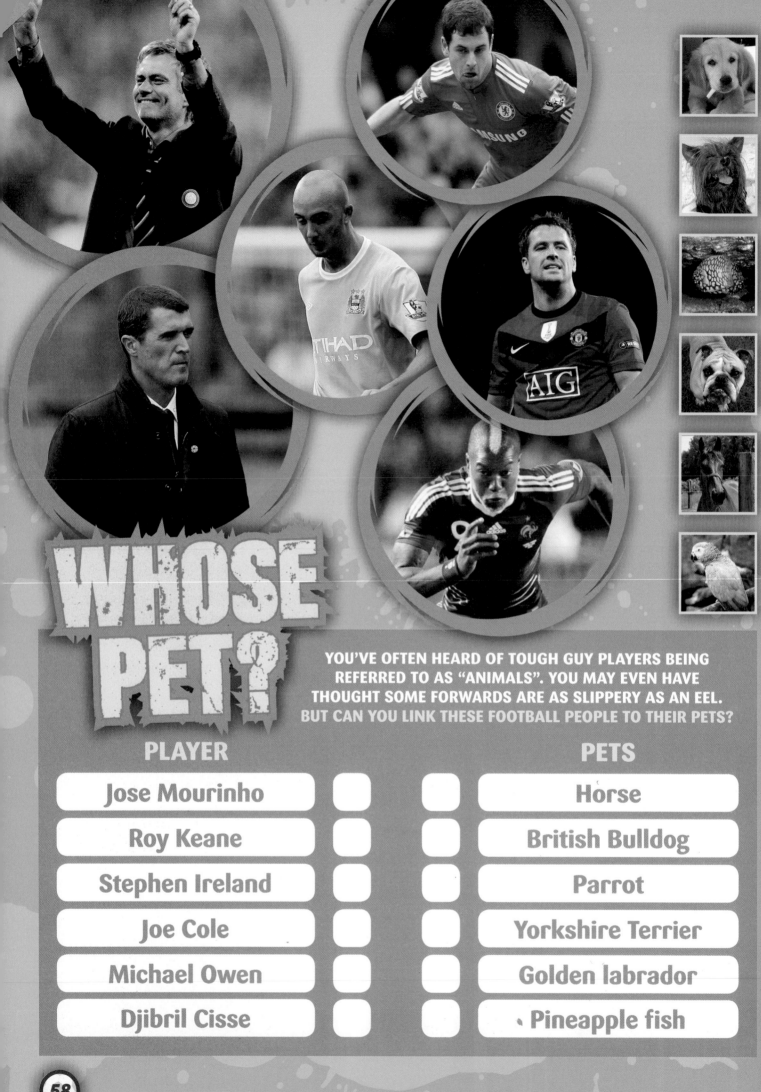

WHOSE PET?

YOU'VE OFTEN HEARD OF TOUGH GUY PLAYERS BEING REFERRED TO AS "ANIMALS". YOU MAY EVEN HAVE THOUGHT SOME FORWARDS ARE AS SLIPPERY AS AN EEL. BUT CAN YOU LINK THESE FOOTBALL PEOPLE TO THEIR PETS?

PLAYER			PETS
Jose Mourinho			Horse
Roy Keane			British Bulldog
Stephen Ireland			Parrot
Joe Cole			Yorkshire Terrier
Michael Owen			Golden labrador
Djibril Cisse			Pineapple fish

YOUR GUIDE TO THE CLUBS

YOUR GUIDE TO THE 20 ENGLISH PREMIER LEAGUES SIDES: PLUS DREAM TEAMS FROM THEIR TOP-FLIGHT YEARS, STATS, FACTS AND INTERVIEWS

Arsenal

PREMIER LEAGUE 2009-10
Position: 3rd
Top scorer:
Cesc Fabregas, 15
Player of the Year:
Cesc Fabregas

FACT FILE
Ground: Emirates Stadium
Capacity: 60,300
Mascot: Gunnersaurus
Premier League best:
Winners, 1998, 2002, 2004
FA Cup winners:
1930, 1936, 1950, 1971,
1979, 1993, 1998, 2002,
2003, 2005

" Confidence comes with winning but my wife will be quick to put me in my place. I think the fans like me more than my wife. **"**
ANDREY ARSHAVIN

ARSENAL

DREAM TEAM by Andrew McCarthy

Thierry Henry's name was first on the team sheet under Wenger and was the first name on mine. Arguably the greatest player to wear the red and white shirt, no player has made a bigger impact than the Frenchman. The club's record marksman with 226 goals, possessed an effortless style and boasted bags of pace.

Ian
Wright
1991-98

Thierry
Henry
1999-07

Dennis
Bergkamp
1995-06

Patrick
Vieira
1996-05

Cesc
Fabregas
2003-

Freddie
Ljungberg
1998-07

Ashley
Cole
1999-06

Tony
Adams
1983-02

Sol
Campbell
2001-06,
2010-

Lee
Dixon
1988-02

David
Seaman
1990-03

SUBS Jens Lehmann 2003-08, Martin Keown 1993-04, Ray Parlour 1992-04, Robert Pires 2000-06, Paul Merson 1985-97

A word or two from...
GAEL CLICHY

Criticism
"Criticism doesn't hurt but if people question your ability you have to ask yourself the question. Of course you can always do better."

Arsene Wenger
"He's the one to give advice and tell you if you are not doing well in training or in a game. I face him every day because even if I have not been playing to my best he is still playing me and that shows he has confidence in me. That's why he earns big money and why we call him the boss."

Losing
"After every defeat you have to dig in and go again. It is only with hard work and a bit of luck that things can happen. You have to ask the right questions of yourself and the team."

Did you know?
Gael loves playing his acoustic guitar and once performed with Roger Daltrey and Pete Townshend of The Who.

PREMIER
LEAGUE
09-10
Position: 6th
Top scorer:
Gabby Agbonlahor, 13
Player of the Year:
James Milner

CLUB FILE
Ground: Villa Park
Capacity: 42,640
Mascot: Hercules,
Bella and Chip
Premier League best:
Runner-up, 1992-93
League winners:
1894-95, 1897, 1905,
1910, 1920, 1957

" For every footballer the aim when they look back on their career is to have a medal to show for it. Ever player in the Premier League will more or less finish their career with enough money and be financially happy. But you have to have silverware to look back on.

RICHARD DUNNE

ASTON VILLA

DREAM TEAM by Tom Vickers

This team has everything: pace, power and precision. Mark Bosnich was a colourful character, elastic between the sticks and his reflexes were outstanding. This back four are legends in the eyes of Villa fans. The midfield is a mix of creation and determination. Ian Taylor is Villa through and through. Up front are two of the most natural finishers ever to strut their stuff at Villa Park.

Dwight Yorke (1989-98)

Dean Saunders (1992-95)

Gareth Barry (1997-09)

Ian Taylor (1994-03)

Paul Merson (1998-02)

Andy Townsend (1993-97)

Alan Wright (1995-03)

Olof Mellberg (2001-08)

Martin Laursen (2004-09)

Paul McGrath (1989-96)

Mark Bosnich (1992-99)

SUBS Gareth Southgate (1995-01), David James (1999-01)
James Milner (2005-06, 08-), Kevin Richardson (1991-95), Dion Dublin (1998-04)

A word or two from... STEWART DOWNING

Changing places
"The boss says I start on the left, Ash [Young] on the right and James [Milner] in the centre but if we want to change it around for five minutes then do it. This works because it gives us a different dimension and creates problems for other teams."

New role
"I am really enjoying it because changing wings and positions means you are always involved in the game. When I joined Villa the manager made it clear that all three of us could play in different positions."

Long-term injury
"It has been frustrating but now it is a great feeling to be playing again. It has gone well for me and I couldn't have had a better start than scoring on my full debut against Portsmouth."

Did you know?
Villa signed Downing from Middlesbrough in summer 2009 for £12m despite the fact he was injured and going to be out of action for quite a time.

BIRMINGHAM CITY
FOOTBALL CLUB
- 1875 -

PREMIER LEAGUE
2009-10
Position: 9th
Top scorer:
Cameron Jerome, 10
Player of the Year:
Joe Hart

FACT FILE
Ground: St. Andrews
Capacity: 30,000
Mascot: Beau Brummie
Premier League best:
9th, 2009-10
FA Cup winners:
Never won

" I'm here to play football and do the best
I can week-in and week-out. I speak to the
gaffer, who asks how it is going, and it
is going well and going smoothly and as
long as it carries on, it will be great. "
LIAM RIDGEWELL

64

BIRMINGHAM CITY

DREAM TEAM by Keith Chambers

I know Joe Hart was only a loan player for us but what a difference he made last season. He was one of the major differences to our side. A ninth-placed finished was good and it was so close to being even better!

Mikael Forssell
2003-08

Christophe Dugarry
2003-04

Stan Lazaridis
199-06

David Dunn
2003-07

Barry Ferguson
2009-

Robbie Savage
2002-05

Martin Grainger
1996-05

Roger Johnson
2009-

Matthew Upson
2003-07

Stephen Carr
2009-

Joe Hart
2009-10

SUBS Emile Heskey 2004-06, Geoff Horsfield 2000-03, Lee Bowyer 2009-, Kenny Cunningham 2002-06, Maik Taylor 2004-

A word or two from... JAMES MCFADDEN

Joining City
"When Alex McLeish took the Birmingham job and came in for me I didn't even need to speak to him. He was gaffer when I was at Motherwell and showed real faith in me with the national side. He is simply a nice guy with talent and know-how."

Reality check
"Nothing puts your feet back on the ground like bathing your kids and changing dirty nappies. But my family and football take up all of my time and I love it."

Errors
"Everyone makes mistakes but if you keep making the same mistakes you need to ask yourself some serious questions. The dressing room here is superb and wants to do so well. Everyone is arguing. It's the same on the training pitch. If someone makes a misplaced pass or is not putting the work in, there are always players ready to jump down their throat."

Did you know?
James was just 19 when he made his Scotland debut in 2002 and now has approaching 50 caps.

BLACKBURN ROVERS F.C.

ARTE ET LABORE

1875

PREMIER LEAGUE
2009-10
Position: 10th
Top scorer:
David Dunn, 9
Player of the Year:
Steven N'Zonzi

FACT FILE
Ground: Ewood Park
Capacity: 31,367
Mascot: Roar the Lion
Premier League best:
Winners, 1995
FA Cup winners:
1884, 1885, 1886,
1890, 1891, 1928

CROWN PAINTS

> **I have played more than I thought I would. It is important to keep training hard and keep learning as much as I can. I think I can get better.**
>
> **STEVEN N'ZONZI**

BLACKBURN ROVERS

DREAM TEAM by Ian Yardley

It would be amiss not to include a number our title-winning squad in this team. Brad Friedel is possibly the best free transfer ever made in the Premier League; Colin Hendry was Braveheart! Shearer is the greatest striker ever produced in this country, his goalscoring record is astounding with headers, free-kicks, penalties, long-range piledrivers, goal poaching... he had it all.

Craig Bellamy (2005–06)

Alan Shearer (1992–96)

Damien Duff (1996–03)

David Bentley (2005–08)

Tugay (2001 – 2009)

David Dunn (1997–03 and 07–)

Colin Hendry (1987–89 and 91–98)

Lucas Neill (2001–07)

Henning Berg (1993–97 and 00–03)

Graeme Le Saux (1993–97)

Brad Friedel (2000–08)

SUBS   Tim Flowers (1993–99), Christopher Samba (2007–), Tim Sherwood (1992–99) Benni McCarthy (2006–10), Roque Santa Cruz (2007–09)

A word or two from...
PAUL ROBINSON

Joining Rovers
"I was ready for a new start and a new challenge. This move has helped me find the fire and ambition that I knew I had but had maybe drained out of me."

Life
"I'm a more rounded person now. I deal with situations a lot better and am more mature. The lessons in life are there to be learned from. And if you don't learn from them, there's no point in having them."

Sam Allardyce
"Maybe some of the fans didn't take to him straight from the beginning, but if you consider what he's done to this club, he has put them back on a platform to being where they were a couple of seasons ago. We have a very good mix of young players and experience."

Did you know?
Robbo has scored two goals in his professional career, one a free-kick from 80-yards. Not bad for a keeper!

BLACKPOOL FOOTBALL CLUB

**CHAMPIONSHIP
2009-10**
Position: 6th,
play-off final winners
Top scorer:
Charlie Adam, 18
Player of the Year:
Charlie Adam

FACT FILE
Ground: Bloomfield Road
Capacity: 12,000
Mascot: Bloomfield Bear
Premier League best:
n/a
FA Cup winners:
1953

> It's one of a kind this club.
> Our budget is probably one of the
> smallest in the league, we wash our own
> kit and clean our own boots, but we are a
> close unit and give 110 percent.
> **IAN EVATT**

BLACKPOOL

THE SQUAD THAT TOOK THEM UP

Blackpool were expected to consolidate their Championship status, as it was just their third season in the second tier since winning the League One play-offs. They didn't have a first-choice keeper – Matthew Gilks and Paul Rachubka each made 20 league appearances. Their highest-scorer was midfielder Charlie Adam, whilst loanee DJ Campbell scored 11 goals in 17 games to ensure promotion.

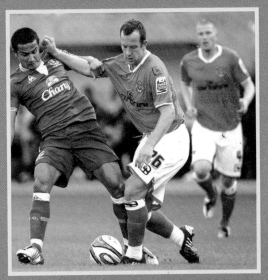

Gary Taylor-Fletcher
(2007 –)

Brett Ormerod
(2008 –)

David Vaughan
(2008 –)

Charlie Adam
(2009 –)

Jason Euell
(2009 –)

Keith Southern
(2002 –)

Neal Eardley
(2009 –)

Alex Baptiste
(2008 –)

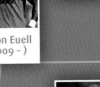
Ian Evatt
(2006 –)

Stephen Crainey
(2007 –)

Matthew Gilks
(2008 –)

SUBS   Paul Rachubka (2007 –), Rob Edwards (2008 –)
Barry Bannan (Loan), Ben Burgess (2006–2010), DJ Campbell (Loan)

A word or two from....
CHARLIE ADAM

Premier League chance
"Hopefully I will become a better player. It will be tough as there are world-class players but I am up for it. We will all have a smile on our faces."

Turning Tangerine
"I came here because Blackpool were the only team to pay the money. I had been on loan and enjoyed it so was more than happy to join. Nobody can take away what we did at Wembley in the play-off final."

Big games
"I've been lucky enough to play some big matches in Europe [for Rangers] and to represent my country [Scotland]. But playing in front of 80,000 at Wembley with an opportunity of being in the Premier League was great."

Winning
"It doesn't matter who you are or what you have done you have to have that hunger to win. Look at Man United with Scholes and Giggs, they are still winning trophies, they still have that drive."

Did you know?
Adam was on loan at St. Mirren and minnows Ross County when he couldn't make the big breakthrough at Rangers – although he played for them in Scottish Cup finals and scored for Gers in the Champions League.

PREMIER
LEAGUE
2009-10
Position: 14th
Top scorer:
Kevin Davies, 9
Player of the Year:
Lee Chung Yong

FACT FILE
Ground: Reebok
Capacity: 28,000
Mascot: Lofty the Lion
Premier League best:
6th, 2005
FA Cup winners:
1923, 1926, 1929, 1958

" As long as I am appreciated
by my manager, team-mates and
the fans then I don't care what
other people think about me.
KEVIN DAVIES "

BOLTON WANDERERS

DREAM TEAM by Ian Chapman

Despite a couple of seasons fighting relegation, Bolton have mostly played watchable football, despite what critics stated. Some outstanding players plied their trade at the Reebok Stadium, and hopefully Owen Coyle can now bring the same flair and a revival.

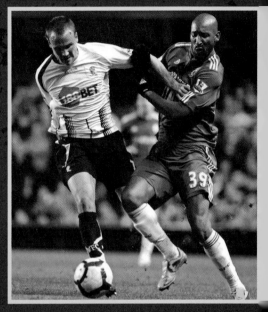

Nicolas Anelka (2006-08)

Kevin Davies (2003-)

Ivan Campo (2003-08)

El-Hadji Diouf (2004-08)

Youri Djorkaeff (2002-04)

Jay-Jay Okocha (2002-06)

Ricardo Gardner (1998-)

Gudni Bergson (1995-03)

Fernado Hierro (2004-05)

Bruno N'Gotty (2001-06)

Jussi Jaaskelainen (1997-)

SUBS John McGinley (1992-96), Michael Ricketts (2000-03), Gary Cahill (2008-), Robbie Elliot (1997-01), Per Frandsen (1996-99 and 00-04).

A word or two from....
MATT TAYLOR

Going north
"I made the right move going to Bolton. I wasn't playing at Portsmouth and I can't sit around on the bench watching football. I need to be playing. What has happened has proved it was the best thing to do."

Good form
"I'm playing as well as I ever have and certainly the best since I've been in the Premier League. I am enjoying my football and that's what its all about for me. I can't wait to put my boots on before every game, it beats the hell out of sitting on your backside, which is what I did too much of during my final days at Portsmouth."

Progress
"When you look at things at the start of the season, it's such a fantastic league and it's such a huge thing financially for the club to stay here. Anything you achieve above that is a bonus. The gap, financially, between the top clubs and ourselves is gigantic but we compete every week and we have done that again."

Did you know?
Matt agreed a three and a half year deal when he joined Wanderers in January 2008 – but then extended it until summer 2012

CHELSEA
FOOTBALL CLUB

**PREMIER
LEAGUE
2009-10**
Position: Champions
Top scorer:
Didier Drogba, 29
Player of the Year:
Didier Drogba

FACT FILE
Ground: Stamford Bridge
Capacity: 41,841
Mascot: Stamford the Lion
Premier League:
Winners: 2005, 2006, 2010
FA Cup winners:
1970, 1997, 2000,
2007, 2009, 2010

" I want to win more trophies and
certainly feel I can do that here.
This is a great club with a great
squad and where the morale is
as high as I've ever experienced.
FRANK LAMPARD

DREAM TEAM by Ben Widger

These players stand out as the most memorable in the years I have followed Chelsea. Not always the longest-serving, certainly in the case of Arjen Robben, however in his first season under Mourinho he was devastating on either wing. Special mention for Dennis Wise who doesn't make this list but started the modern Chelsea era with the cup win in 1997. JT has to be captain.

Gianfranco Zola (1996-03)

Didier Drogba (2004-)

Arjen Robben (2004-07)

Claude Makelele (2003-08)

Frank Lampard (2001-)

Joe Cole (2003-10)

Ashley Cole (2006-)

Marcel Desailly (1998-04)

John Terry (1995-)

Dan Petrescu (1995-00)

* Petr Cech (2004-)

SUBS Carlo Cudicini (1999-09), Ricardo Carvalho (2004-), Graeme Le Saux (1997-03), Gustavo Poyet (1997-01), Mark Hughes (1995-98)

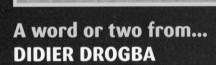

A word or two from... DIDIER DROGBA

Staying put
"When I was saying I wanted to leave even if I went I didn't know if I would find what I have here. I am not scared of a challenge but I don't need a move."

Playing on
"I don't know how long I can continue playing but for me the most important thing is to enjoy being on the pitch. The more games you play the more you learn."

Team work
"Football is a team sport. It is nice to have individual honours but much better when you share the medals with your friends and team-mates. If you work hard something good will happen to you."

Did you know?
The Drog cost Chelsea £24m from Marseille in 2004 - which meant he earned the French side almost £21m in profit, as they bought him from Guingamp for just £3.3m!

Everton

NIL SATIS NISI OPTIMUM

18 78

PREMIER
LEAGUE
2009-10
Position: 8th
Top scorer:
Louis Saha, 13
Player of the Year:
Steven Pienaar

FACT FILE
Ground: Goodison Park
Capacity: 40,157
Mascot: Tiger and Chang
Premier League best:
4th, 2004-05
FA Cup winners:
1906, 1933, 1966,
1984, 1995

> For me it has been one of the best seasons of my life. I have scored more goals than before. I have enjoyed every minute on the pitch with this club.
>
> **DINIYAR BILYALETDINOV**

EVERTON

DREAM TEAM by Paul Carrott

Arguably the most controversial inclusion, but comfortably the most talented, is Wayne Rooney. He joined Everton at the age of ten and quickly tore up the Goodison Park record books. Evertonians revelled in the fact that one of their own was the most talked about talent in world football.

Wayne
Rooney
2002-04

Duncan
Ferguson
94-98, 00-06

Anders
Limpar
1994-97

Tim Cahill
2004-

Mikel Arteta
2005-

Andrei
Kanchelskis
1995-96

Joleon Lescott
2006-09

Phil Jagielka
2007-

Dave Watson
1986-01

Phil Neville
2005-

Neville
Southall
1981-98

SUBS Nigel Martyn 2003-06, David Unsworth 1991-97, 98-04, Marouane Fellaini 2008-, Steven Pienaar 2008-, Peter Beardsley 1991-93

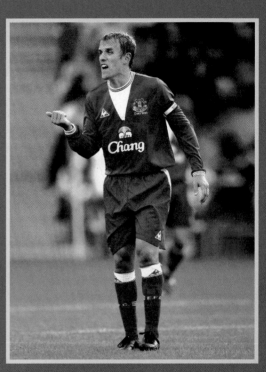

A word or two from...
PHIL NEVILLE

Leaving Old Trafford
"Everything I achieved at United I loved and nobody can take that away. But now I love Everton and you can't compare the two. I never thought when I joined that I would have the special feeling I have now. This place gripped me and I never looked back."

David Moyes
"The manager drives us on all the time. He keeps taking this club to bigger and better things. Everyone knows the gap between the top four and the rest is huge but we are pushing from below. This team can only get better."

After playing
"Coaching or management is my passion. The boss is always on at me to get my badges but I still have plenty of playing ambitions."

Did you know?
Phil won six Premier League titles and three FA Cups during this time at Manchester United. He was on the bench for the club's 1999 Champions League victory.

PREMIER LEAGUE 2009-10
Position: 12th
Top scorer:
Bobby Zamora, 8
Player of the Year:
Bobby Zamora

FACT FILE
Ground: Craven Cottage
Capacity: 25,700
Mascot: Billy the Badger
Premier League best: 7th, 2009
FA Cup winners: Never won

" I think the team spirit and desire is there for all to see. We're certainly not looking downwards, we're definitely looking up. "
DAMIEN DUFF

FULHAM

DREAM TEAM by Luke Sargeant

The front two was no contest. Saha was prolific, scoring 53 goals in 117 appearances. When he left for Old Trafford, McBride became a legend to the Hammersmith End. Van der Sar remains the most accomplished number one the club has ever had, while Danny Murphy captained his side to a European Final.

Brian McBride 2004-08

Louis Saha 2004-08

Luis Boa Morte 2000-07

Sylvain Legwinski 2001-06

Danny Murphy 2007-

Steed Malbranque 2001-06

Paul Konchesky 2007-

Aaron Hughes 2007-

Brede Hangeland 2008-

Steve Finnan 1998-03

Edwin Van der Sar 2001-05

SUBS Mark Schwarzer 2008-, Alain Goma 2001-06, Sean Davis 1996-04, Zoltan Gera 2008-, Bobby Zamora 2008-

A word or two from....
MARK SCHWARZER

Former boss Roy Hodgson
"Roy is one of the best managers I have every worked under. He doesn't just stand around on the touchline barking instructions - he takes 95 per cent of the training himself. That's exceptional for a guy at this level. He's a great guy, a fantastic manager."

Confidence
"Everyone has moments of doubt and I had it. I was only around 21 or 22 in Germany and I did think it wasn't going to work out. But you have to stay focused and consistent. I did that and it worked out for me."

Oz league
"I am very happy that the game has picked up and that it is so popular in Australia. It is great for all the young players coming through and who are trying to earn a place in the international team. I grew up playing in the old league in Australia and we were getting crowds of 7,000 to 8,000 and it dropped off dramatically. But to see them getting regular crowds of 30,000-40,000 is frightening."

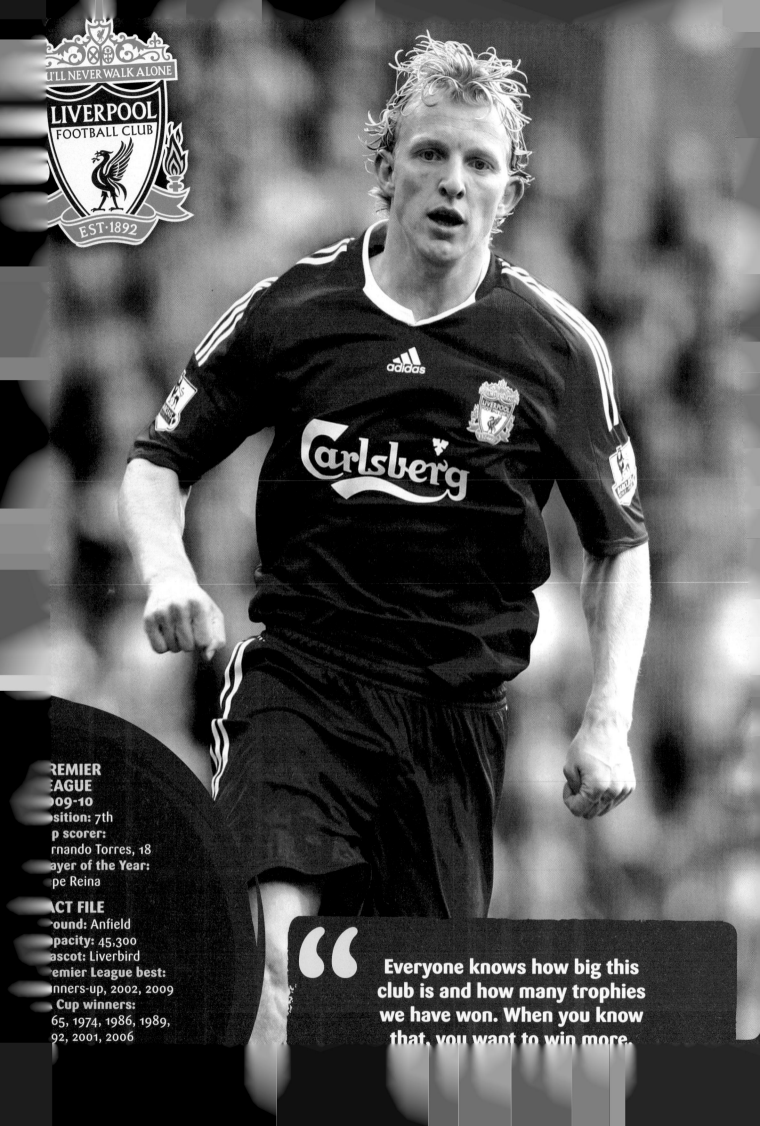

LIVERPOOL FOOTBALL CLUB
U'LL NEVER WALK ALONE
EST·1892

REMIER
EAGUE
009-10
sition: 7th
p scorer:
rnando Torres, 18
ayer of the Year:
pe Reina

ACT FILE
ound: Anfield
pacity: 45,300
ascot: Liverbird
emier League best:
nners-up, 2002, 2009
Cup winners:
65, 1974, 1986, 1989,
92, 2001, 2006

" Everyone knows how big this
club is and how many trophies
we have won. When you know
that, you want to win more.

LIVERPOOL

DREAM TEAM by Phillip Reviere

Every generation has its icon, and one of Liverpool's most famous icons - over all generations - has undoubtedly been Kenny Dalglish. He amassed 515 appearances and notched 172 goals in a long and distinguished career.

Kenny
Dalglish
1977-1990

Ian Rush
1980-1987,
1988-1996

John
Barnes
1987-1997

Jan
Molby
1984-1996

Steven
Gerrard
1998-

Steve
McManaman
1990-1999

John
Arne Riise
2001-2008

Sami
Hyypia
1999-2009

Jamie
Carragher
1996-

Steve
Nicol
1981-1995

Bruce
Grobbelaar
1981-1994

A word or two from....
PEPE REINA

Being Red
"I am very proud to play for Liverpool. Everybody knows what it is to play for Liverpool. It's a pleasure and a tremendous honour. Some things in a player's career should be more important than money."

Title hunts
"At Liverpool you have to be fighting for the title and that's what we will be doing. We are involved in many competitions and just targeting one of them is not enough. The Premier League would definitely be best."

Personal tributes
"I appreciate all the nice things people have said about me but I feel I have improved many things in my game at Liverpool. I still have plenty of things to learn and a long way to go - hopefully that will be with Liverpool."

Did you know?
Pepe's father Miguel was also a goalkeeper and played for Atletico Madrid. He was twice voted best keeper in La Liga.

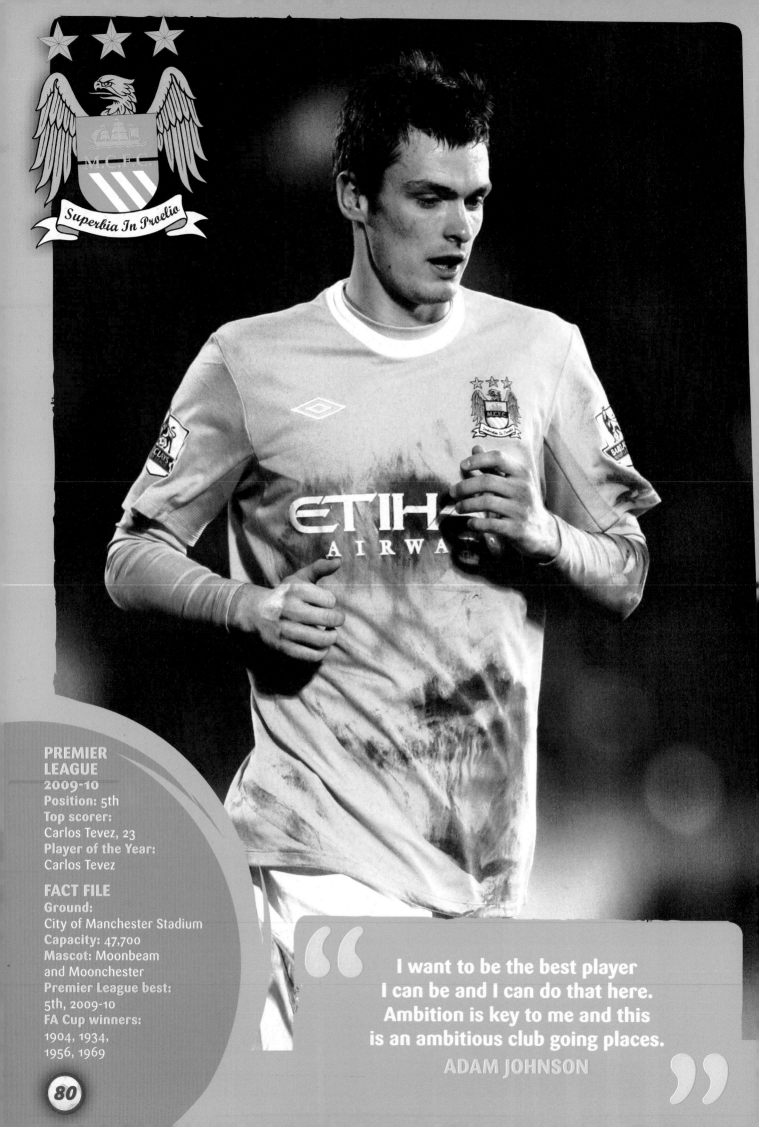

PREMIER LEAGUE
2009-10
Position: 5th
Top scorer:
Carlos Tevez, 23
Player of the Year:
Carlos Tevez

FACT FILE
Ground:
City of Manchester Stadium
Capacity: 47,700
Mascot: Moonbeam
and Moonchester
Premier League best:
5th, 2009-10
FA Cup winners:
1904, 1934,
1956, 1969

Superbia In Proelio

"
I want to be the best player
I can be and I can do that here.
Ambition is key to me and this
is an ambitious club going places.
ADAM JOHNSON
„

MANCHESTER CITY

DREAM TEAM by Mike Wood

As City finished in fifth in 2009-10, their highest position since the Premier League began, I have based my team around the current squad with a few favourites thrown in. Our previous best finish was ninth in 2007-08.

Andy Cole
2005-06

Carlos Tevez
2009-

Craig Bellamy
2009-

Joey Barton
2002-07

Gareth Barry
2009-

Shaun Wright-Phillips
1999-05, 08-

Danny Tiatto
1998-04

Kolo Toure
2009-

Richard Dunne
2000-09

Vedran Corluka
2007-08

Shay Given
2009-

SUBS Georgi Kinkladze 1995-98, Martin Petrov 2007-, Nicolas Anelka 2002-04, Emmanuel Adebayor 2009-, Stephen Ireland 2005-

A word or two from....
SHAY GIVEN

Being City
"When players come up against Man City now it's a really big carrot for them to beat us. We've got to love that. We are progressing for sure, but we want to keep progressing and become better and stronger."

Chasing United
"Look across Manchester and see Sir Alex Ferguson and the stability and success Man United have had under him which is phenomenal. If you want to have a successful team it definitely works that way."

Moving from Tyneside
"Newcastle fans are very passionate, there is a lot of pressure there as football is a religion. But we are also under a lot of pressure here to produce. We have a real chance of winning something and that is why I came here."

Did you know?
Shay, who lost his mother to cancer when he was a boy, is a massive supporter of charities that help fight the horrible disease.

MANCHESTER UNITED

PREMIER LEAGUE
2009-10
Position: Runner-up
Top scorer:
Wayne Rooney, 26
Player of the Year:
Wayne Rooney

FACT FILE
Ground:
Old Trafford
Capacity: 76,200
Mascot: Fred the Red
Premier League best:
Winners: 1993, 1994, 1996,
1997, 1999, 2000, 2001, 2003,
2007, 2008, 2009
FA Cup winners:
1909, 1948, 1963, 1977, 1983, 1985,
1990, 1994, 1996, 1999, 2004

" When it comes to records I have done my best to play things down. Winning trophies matters most, it's as simple as that. If I pass milestones in the meantime then great. "

MANCHESTER UNITED

DREAM TEAM by Jon Reeves

No Beckham and Rooney on the bench. That says a lot about the players who have been part of Man United. Ronaldo shades out Beckham as when he left United after six years he was one of the best players in the world.

Eric Cantona
1992-1997

Mark Hughes
1988-1995

Ryan Giggs
1990-

Roy Keane
1993-2005

Paul Scholes
1994-

Cristiano Ronaldo
2003-2009

Patrice Evra
2006-

Jaap Stam
1998-2001

Rio Ferdinand
2002-

Denis Irwin
1990-2002

Peter Schmeichel
1991-1999

SUBS Edwin van der Sar 2005-, Gary Neville 1992-, Nemanja Vidic 2006-, Ole Gunnar Solskjaer 1996-07, Wayne Rooney 2004-

A word or two from.... ANTONIO VALENCIA

Battling
"I am happy with my work in the team, I know I must fight every day for my place. It's not easy to get into the starting XI here, but that is my challenge."

Dreams
"I always dream of being at a big club and to win titles, now I can fulfill those dreams at United. The coach insisted he wanted me and that came as a real surprise. From the moment I joined it was clear, he explained why United needed me. Mr Ferguson is very open and gives you a chance."

Ronaldo...
"Cristiano is a superstar and I'm Valencia, a footballer learning each day. We are different players."

Did you know?
Valencia was Man of the Match in the 2010 League Cup Final, a game in which he set up Wayne Rooney's winning goal.

NEWCASTLE UNITED

HAMPIONSHIP
09-10
sition: Champions
p scorers:
vin Nolan and
dy Carroll, both 17
yer of the Year:
vin Nolan

CT FILE
ound: St. James' Park
pacity: 52,387
scot:
ggie and Monty Magpie
emier League Best:
d, 1996, 1997
Cup winners:
0, 1924, 1932,
1, 1952, 1955

"We worked hard to get the big fixtures back. You want to be going to Old Trafford and Stamford Bridge and you want to test yourselves against the best players.

NEWCASTLE UNITED

DREAM TEAM by Glenn Mitchell

It was difficult to leave Steve Harper on the bench, likewise to leave out Phillipe Albert. There was only one choice as the main striker – shame we didn't keep Sir Les longer. Jonas and Jose got the nod as they work so well on the left.

Alan Shearer
1996-2006

Les Ferdinand
1995-97

Jonas Gutierrez
2008-

Peter Beardsley
1993-1997

Gary Speed
1998-2004

Nobby Solano
98-04, 05-07

Jose Enrique
2007-

Steven Taylor
2003-

Aaron Hughes
1997-2005

Warren Barton
1995-2001

Shay Given
1997-2009

SUBS Steve Harper 1993-, James Milner 2004-2008, Phillipe Albert 1994-99, Tino Asprilla 1996-1998, Rob Lee 1992-2002

A word or two from...
JOSE ENRIQUE

Staying at St. James'
"I'm so happy I decided to stay at Newcastle. I love the city and the club. All the foreign players hate the weather here, but it's not jus Newcastle, it's England. I'm really settled here and I have no desire to go back to Spain. I'm happy at Newcastle. In my three seasons here I know the fans like me and I love that. That is more important for me than anything else, more important than trophies and cups."

Improving
"I think I am a better player now than I was when I played that first game in the Championship, the experience will benefit me in the long term. I feel I have played wel and become stronger. It is different to the Premier League, but it has given me more confidence in English football."

Being relegated
"When I signed we were a club who were looking to play in Europe. I hope to help Newcastle go back to that level. I don't want to think too much about relegation, it was a very bad experience. I think it will always stay with me."

Did you know?
Jose struggled when he first arrived at the Toon under Sam Allardyce – now the fans sing "Jose, Jose, Jose, Jose..."

STOKE CITY
1863
THE POTTERS

PREMIER LEAGUE
2009-10
Position: 11th
Top scorer:
Matthew Etherington, 5
Player of the Year:
Matthew Etherington

FACT FILE
Ground: Britannia Stadium
Capacity: 28,383
Mascot: Pottermus
Premier League best:
11th, 2009-10
FA Cup winners:
0

" The bottom line is that I am happy in my life. I'm storing all the man-of-match awards at home. There are a few there! I let my girlfriend drink them.
MATTHEW ETHERINGTON "

STOKE CITY

DREAM TEAM by Neil Chadwick

As a current season ticket holder, I've been a Potters' fan for over 30 years now, despite living in or around London for most of those – every home match involves a round trip of over 300 miles. Most of my team picks itself given we've only been in the division for two seasons. It's mainly last season's best line-up, apart from James Beattie whose goals kept us up in 2009-10.

James Beattie
(2009-)

Ricardo Fuller
(2006-)

Matthew Etherington
(2009-)

Glen Whelan
(2008-)

Dean Whitehead
(2009-)

Rory Delap
(2006-)

Danny Higginbotham
(2006-)

Ryan Shawcross
(2007-)

Abdoulaye Faye
(2008-)

Andy Wilkinson
(2001-)

Thomas Sorensen
(2008-)

SUBS Asmir Begovic (2010-), Robert Huth (2009-), Liam Lawrence (2006-), Tuncay (2009-), Mamady Sidibe (2005-)

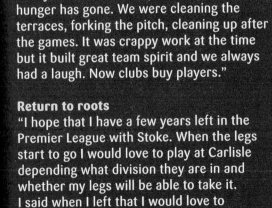

A word or two from...
RORY DELAP

City life
"We've had the odd little bad run here and there but since then it has been improving every season. Any team that gets promotion to the Premier League has to look at staying in the league and the aim is to stay for two, three, four seasons until it becomes possible to break into the top eight."

Young players
"They don't have to do jobs. Maybe the hunger has gone. We were cleaning the terraces, forking the pitch, cleaning up after the games. It was crappy work at the time but it built great team spirit and we always had a laugh. Now clubs buy players."

Return to roots
"I hope that I have a few years left in the Premier League with Stoke. When the legs start to go I would love to play at Carlisle depending what division they are in and whether my legs will be able to take it. I said when I left that I would love to return and that hasn't changed."

Did you know?
Rory started his career at Carlisle and has now played more than 100 games each for Derby, Southampton and Stoke, plus a short spell at Sunderland.

PREMIER LEAGUE
2009-10
Position: 13th
Top scorer:
Darren Bent, 24
Player of the Year:
Darren Bent

FACT FILE
Ground: Stadium of Light
Capacity: 49,000
Mascot: Samson and Delilah
Premier League best:
7th, 2000, 2001
FA Cup winners:
1937, 1973

"
It's the life of the goalkeeper,
one mistake and you're back
in the depths again. I have
to guard against that.
CRAIG GORDON

SUNDERLAND

DREAM TEAM by Jimmy Pugh

Kevin Phillips will forever be a hero on Wearside, not just because he scored that winner against Newcastle in 1999. Phillips and Niall Quinn, his strike partner, developed a formidable partnership. In 1999-2000, "Super Kev" scored 30 league goals to win the European Golden Boot.

Niall Quinn
1996-02

Kevin Phillips
1997-03

Julio Arca
2000-06

Kevin Ball
1990-99

Stefan Schwarz
1999-03

Nicky Summerbee
1997-01

Michael Gray
1992-04

Paul Butler
1998-00

Stanislav Varga
00-03, 06-08

Nyron Nosworthy
2005-10

Lionel Perez
1996-98

SUBS Thomas Sorensen 1998-03, George McCartney 1998-06, 08-, Alex Rae 1996-01, Dean Whitehead 2004-09, Michael Bridges 1995-99, 04-05

A word or two from....
KIERAN RICHARDSON

England
"I have had a taste of it and I want to play for England again but that can only come from playing well for my club and playing in every game. Hopefully I will get there."

Sunderland
"This is a massive club and we met the owner and he told us he wants the club to move forward and he wants the best players to make progress. It's what you want to hear as a player."

Playing
"When you are not playing regularly it does affect your confidence. But the good thing about football is that you've always got the next game to put it right. When you're not getting a lot of action, you do tend to get frustrated, but you've just got to keep your head down and keep going. I've got a great family behind me who support me and give me the confidence I need."

Did you know?
A painting Kieran did of the Manchester skyline hangs up in Sir Alex Ferguson's office at Old Trafford. The player presented it to the gaffer when he left United.

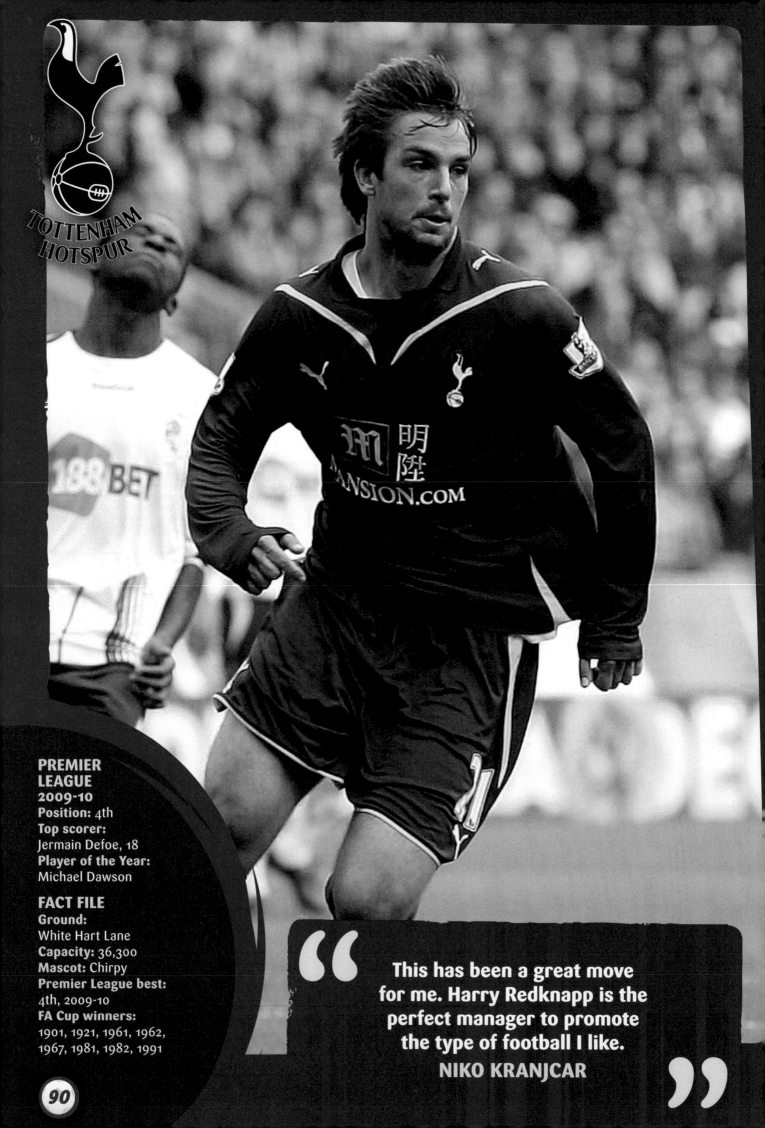

TOTTENHAM HOTSPUR

PREMIER LEAGUE 2009-10
Position: 4th
Top scorer:
Jermain Defoe, 18
Player of the Year:
Michael Dawson

FACT FILE
Ground:
White Hart Lane
Capacity: 36,300
Mascot: Chirpy
Premier League best:
4th, 2009-10
FA Cup winners:
1901, 1921, 1961, 1962,
1967, 1981, 1982, 1991

90

" **This has been a great move for me. Harry Redknapp is the perfect manager to promote the type of football I like.**
NIKO KRANJCAR "

TOTTENHAM HOTSPUR

DREAM TEAM by Chris Thomas

So often known as "The Perennial Underachievers", looking at this side it may be hard to see why Tottenham have flattered to deceive since the inception of the Premier League. Sol Campell's in there – I've not forgiven him for the move to our biggest rivals, just grudgingly accepted his quality!

Teddy
Sheringham
(1992-97, 2001-03)

Jurgen
Klinsmann
(1994-95, 97-98)

David Ginola
(1997-00)

Gus Poyet
(2001-04)

Gheorghe
Popescu
(1994-95)

Darren
Anderton
(1992-04)

Mauricio
Taricco
(1999-04)

Ledley King
(1999-)

Sol Campbell
(1992-01)

Stephen Carr
(1993-04)

Neil Sullivan
(2000-02)

SUBS Heurelho Gomes (2008-), Gary Mabbutt (1982-98)
Robbie Keane (2002-08, 09-), Simon Davies (2000-05), Steffen Freund (1999-03)

A word or two from....
JERMAIN DEFOE

Improving
"I want to be the best otherwise there is no point. I might as well stay at home and watch it on the TV. If the goals dried up tomorrow the last thing I would do is sit back and think I had done enough. Even if I score four goals in my next England game it means nothing if I don't get things right for Tottenham."

Harry Redknapp
"He is unbelievable, one of those managers if you are good enough you will play, it doesn't matter how old you are."

Sending off v Portsmouth
"My mum said she didn't want to see it on TV because she would give me a bit of a mouthful. My grandad saw it and gave me a bit of stick. It was silly and something that won't happen again."

Did you know?
Jermain has a small gym at home where he takes out his aggression on a punchbag. One of his heroes is Arsenal legend Ian Wright who offers him advice.

WEST BROMWICH ALBION

CHAMPIONSHIP
2009-10
Position: Runner-up
Top scorer:
Graham Dorrans and
Chris Brunt, both 13
Player of the Year:
Graham Dorrans

FACT FILE
Ground: The Hawthorns
Capacity: 26,500
Mascot: Baggie Bird
and Baggie Bird Junior
Premier League:
17th, 2004-05
FA Cup winners:
1888, 1892, 1931,
1954, 1968

> " There are a few people at the
> club with a point to prove after
> getting relegated last time. When
> something goes against you that
> is how you should react. "
> **CHRIS BRUNT**

WEST BROMWICH ALBION

DREAM TEAM by Neil Lee

This is a team full of great memories for me, including Igor Balis scoring the penalty that more or less sent us up in 2002! Some of this side were under-rated: Russell Hoult should have played for England and Thomas Gaardsøe never got the credit he deserved before his career was curtailed by injury (though he has recently returned to football!). Graham Dorrans is the best midfielder we've had at the Albion since Bryan Robson.

Kevin Phillips (2006-08)

Bob Taylor (1992-98 and 00-03)

Graham Dorrans (2008 -)

Robert Koren (2007-10)

Derek McInnes (2000-03)

Jason Koumas (2002-07)

Neil Clement (2000-10)

Thomas Gaardsøe (2003-06)

Darren Moore (2001-06)

Igor Balis 2000-03)

Russell Hoult (2001-07)

SUBS Alan Miller (1991 and 97-00), Zoltan Gera (2004-08), Lee Hughes (1997-01), Richard Sneekes (1996-01), Kevin Campbell (2005-06).

A word or two from....
ROMAN BEDNAR

Promotion
"I want to play in the Premier League for the rest of my life and I will do anything to do that. All the games in the Premier League are big. We want to compete with the best players in the world."

Being a Baggie
"This club is always under pressure because we are always looking to get promoted or trying not to get relegated. That's why I love this club. It makes you work really hard. Of course the target is to stay up."

Pleasing people
"The gaffer, players, supporters, the club – they are the most important thing. That's all I need to worry about. The future is the most important."

New players
"It's always better for the team if you have a good squad and if the gaffer brings in more competition I don't mind. If I'm not going to play then I will be disappointed and do something about it."

Did you know?
Roman is an international for the Czech Republic and cost West Brom £2.3m when he signed from Hearts in summer 2008.

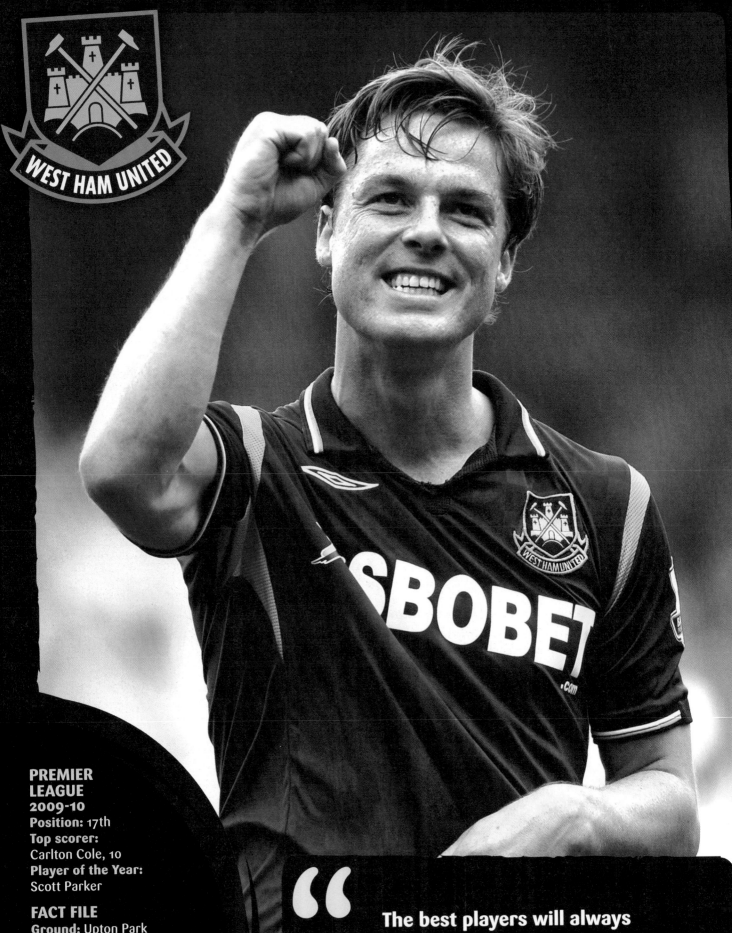

WEST HAM UNITED

PREMIER LEAGUE 2009-10
Position: 17th
Top scorer:
Carlton Cole, 10
Player of the Year:
Scott Parker

FACT FILE
Ground: Upton Park
Capacity: 35,100
Mascot: Herbie the Hammer
Premier League best:
5th 1999
FA Cup winners:
1964, 1975, 1980

> " The best players will always come through. I don't compare myself with them. I just concentrate on myself. I know what I'm good at, I know what my attributes are. "
>
> **SCOTT PARKER**

94

WEST HAM UNITED

DREAM TEAM by Steve Larking

Paolo Di Canio was perhaps the most gifted player to ever wear the Claret and Blue of West Ham. He was the archetypal troubled genius signed by Harry Redknapp. Goal of the season in 2000 for the cheekiest of volleys and the 2001 fair play award were the redemption that Paolo deserved.

Paolo Di Canio
1999-03

Tony Cottee
1994-96

Joe Cole
1998-03

John Moncur
1994-03

Michael Carrick
1998-2004

Trevor Sinclair
1998-03

Julian Dicks
89-93, 94-99

Rio Ferdinand
1995-00

Slaven Bilic
1996-97

Tomas Repka
2001-06

Ludek Miklosko
1990-98

SUBS Rob Green 2006-, Scott Parker 2007-, Alvin Martin 1977-96, Ian Bishop 1989-98, Trevor Morley 1989-95

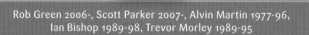

A word or two from... ZAVON HINES

His aims

"I just want to keep on scoring goals and progressing. People have started recognising me in the streets. I can cope with the limelight but I will keep my head down and keep learning. Seeing the players out there playing and the way the fans are towards the players when they're winning just makes me want to play even more."

His inspirations

"Gianfranco Zola was a hero of mine as a kid, I used to watch him on the TV and he was brilliant. Carlton Cole has been great to me. He inspires me and it has been great to be involved with England Under-21s."

His country

"I still have family out there but playing for Jamaica has not been on my mind. The manager [of Jamaica] called me up and told me he wanted me in the squad. I felt good. My faith is also important to me. I do go to church and I do believe in God."

Did you know?

Hines, born in Jamaica, grew up in London's East End and came through the famed West Ham Academy. His progress has been hampered by a couple of knee injuries.

WIGAN ATHLETIC
1932

PREMIER LEAGUE 2009-10
Position: 16th
Top scorer:
Hugo Rodallega, 10
Player of the Year:
Charles N'Zogbia

FACT FILE
Ground: DW Stadium
Capacity: 24,826
Mascot: Stripey the Laticat
Premier League:
10th, 2006
FA Cup winners:
0

> " I love it in England and in the Premier League. I want to concentrate on staying fit and getting in the side on a regular basis and help to push the club to the next level. "
> **STEVE GOHOURI**

WIGAN ATHLETIC

DREAM TEAM by Simon Gregory

This team shows Wigan's meteoric rise though the Premier League. There are players from our first season which led to a top 10 finish and a Carling Cup final appearance; to those who kept us in the league over the years; through to those who are taking the club forward. If this team played under current manager Roberto Martinez then a top half finish would be almost certain.

Hugo
Rodallega
(2009-)

Jason
Roberts
(2004-06)

Charles
N'Zogbia
(2009-)

Wilson
Palacios
(2008-09)

Jimmy
Bullard
(2003-06)

Luis Antonio
Valencia
(2006-09)

Leighton
Baines
(2002-07)

Titus
Bramble
(2007-)

Arjan
DeZeeuw
(1999-02, 05-07)

Pascal
Chimbonda
(2005-06)

Mike Pollitt
(2005-)

SUBS Chris Kirkland (2006-), David Unsworth (2007), Paul Scharner (2006-)
Maynor Figueroa (2008-), Lee McCulloch (2001-07), Emile Heskey (2006-09)

A word or two from...
GARY CALDWELL

Joining Wigan
"I feel like I'm coming into the best years of my career - as a defender once you get into your thirties I think you do your best stuff. Hopefully Wigan have got my best years and I'll do well for the club."

Wigan boss Roberto Martinez
"The manager is really positive and gives us the confidence to go and play. He made it quite clear what his ambitions are for this club and how much he wanted to bring me here."

Scotland boss Craig Levein
"If you look at Craig's track record, it's easy to see why the SFA appointed him. I hope he can lead us to a finals. From what I'm told, he's the type of manager you want to play for and that's important. He's a no-nonsense type and will have the squad's respect."

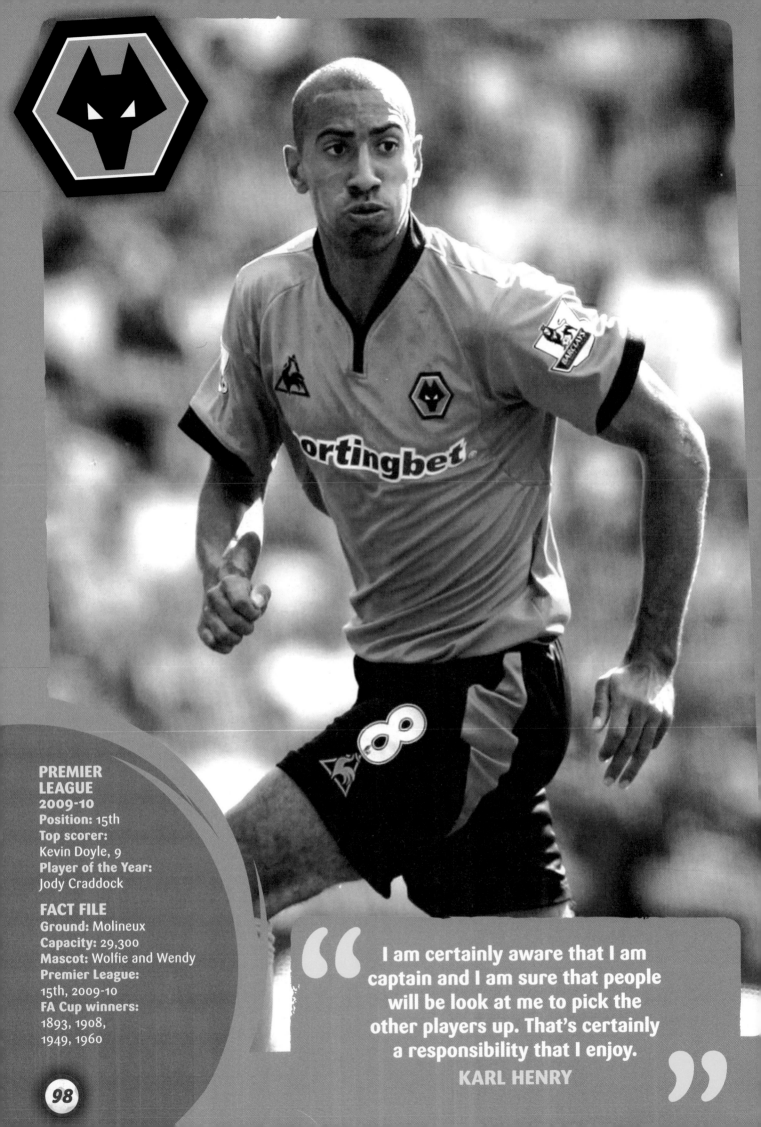

PREMIER LEAGUE 2009-10
Position: 15th
Top scorer:
Kevin Doyle, 9
Player of the Year:
Jody Craddock

FACT FILE
Ground: Molineux
Capacity: 29,300
Mascot: Wolfie and Wendy
Premier League:
15th, 2009-10
FA Cup winners:
1893, 1908,
1949, 1960

" I am certainly aware that I am captain and I am sure that people will be look at me to pick the other players up. That's certainly a responsibility that I enjoy. "

KARL HENRY

WOLVERHAMPTON WANDERERS

DREAM TEAM by Pete Cashmore

Did we really once have Steve Bull and Robbie Keane in the same team? Apparently we did – AND Don Goodman too. Robbie will have to be happy warming the bench though, something he gets plenty of practice at nowadays. Thomas gets the captain's armband in recognition of what he has done outside of the game. Thanks to Stephen Hunt's signing, the left-wing slot is a problem no more...

Kevin Doyle
(2009-)

Steve Bull
(1986-99)

Stephen Hunt
(2010-)

Paul Ince
(2002-06)

Geoff Thomas
(1993-97)

Michael Kightly
(2007-)

Lee Naylor
(1997-2006)

Jody Craddock
(2003-)

Joleon Lescott
(2000-06)

Denis Irwin
(2002-04)

Marcus Hahnemann
(2009-)

SUBS Robbie Keane (1997-99), Colin Cameron (2001-06) Kenny Miller (2001-06), Mark Kennedy (2001-06), Kevin Muscat (1997-02)

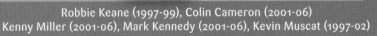

A word or two from....
MATT JARVIS

Starting out
"My brother got scouted by Millwall playing for Epsom Eagles and I got picked up the same way. We were both released but I got picked up by Gillingham. My brother isn't in football now as he got injured that's why every game you play you want to play as well as you can for as long as you can."

Hero
"Ryan Giggs is my hero. As a kid I went to Southampton and got a photo taken with him. When fans ask for their picture with me I just think wow, it's great."

Battling for a place
"We have got a strong squad now and you have to take your chance when it comes along. You had to keep your levels extremely high before and with the strengthening of the squad that's even more the case now. There is a big squad with everyone fighting to keep hold of their shirt and the need to play well otherwise you won't be in the team."

Did you know?
Matt's a bit of a sports expert having represented his school at football, swimming, cross-country and table tennis!

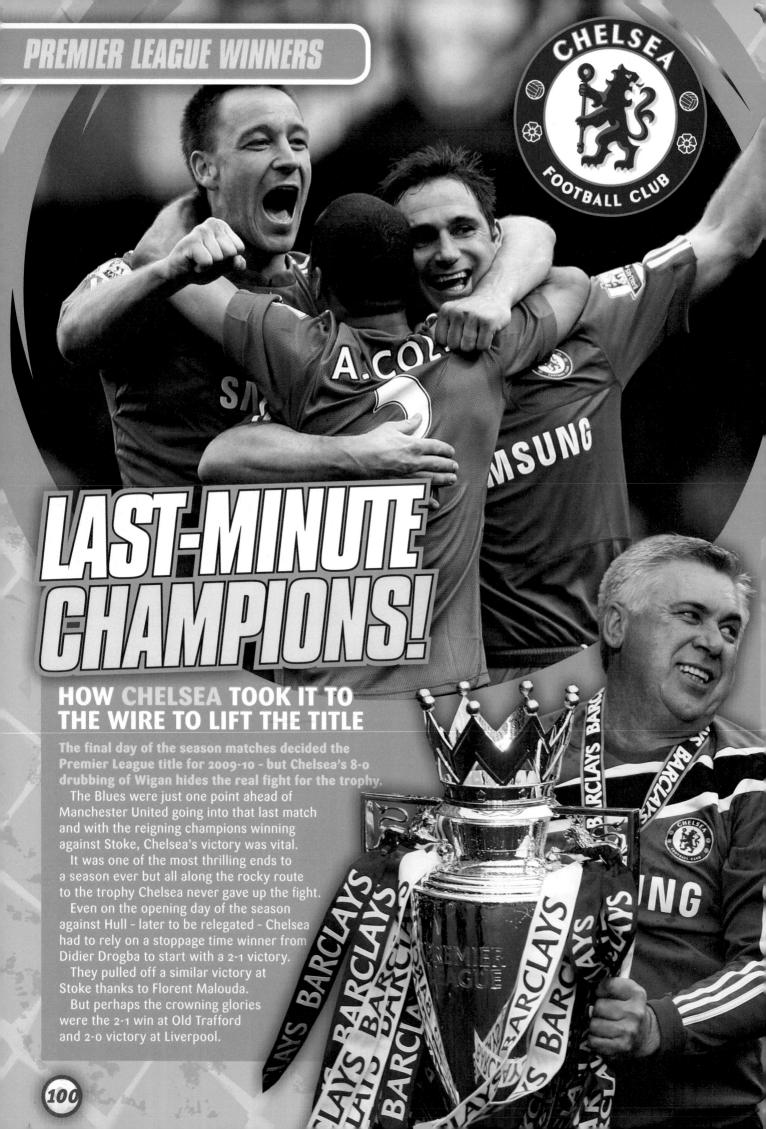

LAST-MINUTE CHAMPIONS!

HOW CHELSEA TOOK IT TO THE WIRE TO LIFT THE TITLE

The final day of the season matches decided the Premier League title for 2009-10 - but Chelsea's 8-0 drubbing of Wigan hides the real fight for the trophy.

The Blues were just one point ahead of Manchester United going into that last match and with the reigning champions winning against Stoke, Chelsea's victory was vital.

It was one of the most thrilling ends to a season ever but all along the rocky route to the trophy Chelsea never gave up the fight.

Even on the opening day of the season against Hull - later to be relegated - Chelsea had to rely on a stoppage time winner from Didier Drogba to start with a 2-1 victory.

They pulled off a similar victory at Stoke thanks to Florent Malouda.

But perhaps the crowning glories were the 2-1 win at Old Trafford and 2-0 victory at Liverpool.

WHAT THEY SAID

⚽ John Terry, skipper: "This feels magnificent. We have got the title back and we need to do what Man United have done and maintain it for a few years. I've been hurting watching them win it for the past three years."

⚽ Carlo Ancelotti, manager: "I think this title could be the first of many because we have a very good squad for next year and the years after. I remember every victory. We are champions of the best league in the world."

⚽ Didier Drogba, top scorer: "This is the best moment I have had since I became a professional footballer. We scored a lot of goals and we have played some good football. The team have worked hard for this all season."

FACT FILE

⚽ Chelsea banked £53.6m for their title win - £26.7m for taking part, £10.9m for live TV appearances and £16m for finishing top.

⚽ Carlo Ancelotti is the first Italian to win the Premier League. It has also been won by two Scots (Sir Alex Ferguson and Kenny Dalglish), a Frenchman (Arsene Wenger) and a Portugal-born boss (Jose Mourinho).

⚽ Manchester City were the only side to complete a double over Chelsea during the season.

⚽ Didier Drogba scored a total of 36 goals - 29 of them in the Premier League. That made him only the fourth player to win the Premiership Golden Boot more than once.

TALE OF THE TABLES

How the top of the Premier League has looked each time Chelsea have won their titles

2005	P	W	GF	GA	PTS
Chelsea	38	29	72	15	95
Arsenal	38	25	87	36	83
Man United	38	22	58	26	77
Everton	38	18	45	46	61

2006	P	W	GF	GA	PTS
Chelsea	38	29	72	22	91
Man United	38	25	72	34	83
Liverpool	38	25	57	25	82
Arsenal	38	20	68	31	67

2010	P	W	GF	GA	PTS
Chelsea	38	27	103	32	86
Man United	38	27	86	28	85
Arsenal	38	23	83	41	75
Tottenham	38	21	67	41	70

MAGPIES FLY HIGH

NEWCASTLE UNITED
SOAR BACK TO THE PREMIER LEAGUE

On May 24, 2009 Newcastle fans were crying in their flat Brown Ale as the club hit the rocks.

Their failure to pick up just one point at Aston Villa meant they were relegated to English football's second-tier for the first time in 17 years.

On April 5, 2010, the Brown Ale was fizzing and flowing freely as the Geordies cemented their return to the top-flight – before their 2-1 home win against Sheffield United, as Nottingham Forest had failed to win against Cardiff.

And on April 19, the side's fans were soaring high above the Tyne as they celebrated winning the Championship, thanks to a 2-0 victory at Plymouth.

They had started the season without a permanent manager as legend Alan Shearer handed the reins back to Chris Hughton to once again be caretaker.

Newcastle owner Mike Ashley was still attempting to sell the club and there was complete turmoil around St. James' Park. But quiet man Hughton just got on with his job and won Manager of the Month awards for August, September and November which earned him a crack at the manager's job on a permanent basis.

His steadying influence was reflected in a string of great results on the pitch and there was further stability when the owner declared the club was no longer for sale.

Hughton, the former Tottenham and Republic of Ireland defender said: "It's an incredibly proud moment for me, it was a long and tough season. It's a very strange thing to say but winning the title is almost as important as going up.

"I'm very proud of this group of lads and the way they've gone about their business. Whenever we've had a blip they've generally come back firing."

PROMOTION POINTS

⚽ Newcastle ended the season on an incredible unbeaten 17-match run.

⚽ Keeper Steve Harper celebrated his first full season as the side's No.1 with a club record 22 clean sheets.

⚽ Striker Shola Ameobi hit his first-ever hat-trick for the club in a 3-0 home win over Reading.

⚽ The 52,181 crowd for the last home game of the season against Ipswich was a Championship record.

⚽ United were unbeaten at home all season and didn't suffer a defeat whilst playing in their traditional black and white stripes.

CHAMPIONSHIP FINAL TABLE

01	Newcastle United	46	55	102
02	West Brom	46	41	91
03	Nottingham Forest	46	25	79
04	Cardiff city	46	19	76
05	Leicester City	46	16	76
06	Blackpool	46	16	70
07	Swansea city	46	3	69
08	Sheffield United	46	7	65
09	Reading	46	5	63
10	Bristol City	46	-9	63
11	Middlesbrough	46	8	62
12	Doncaster Rovers	46	1	60
13	Queens Park Rangers	46	-7	57
14	Derby County	46	-10	56
15	Ipswich Town	46	-11	56
16	Watford	46	-7	54
17	Preston North End	46	-15	54
18	Barnsley	46	-16	54
19	Coventry City	46	-17	54
20	Scunthorpe United	46	-22	52
21	Crystal Palace	46	-3	49
22	Sheffield Wednesday	46	-20	47
23	Plymouth Argyle	46	-25	41
24	Peterborough United	46	-34	34

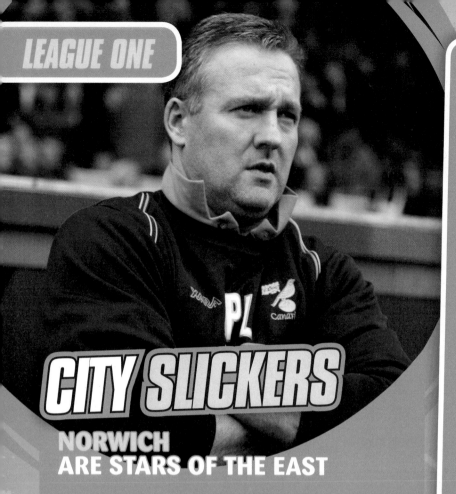

CITY SLICKERS

NORWICH ARE STARS OF THE EAST

Even the most die-hard Norwich City fans must have wondered what the campaign held for their side when the Canaries were hammered 7-1 at home by Colchester on the first day of the 2009-10 season.

It was the first time in 49 years that they had slumped to the third-tier of English football and things looked bleak.

Club legend Bryan Gunn was in charge for just the first week and was replaced by Colchester boss Paul Lambert.

That proved their most inspired move of the season as the former Celtic and Scotland midfielder (above) led his side to a clear title win.

And what's more, they did it in style! They bounced back at the first attempt thanks to a glut of goals and attacking play.

Lambert admitted: "The lads have been absolutely great, every game they've given every effort and some top-class performances and those people behind me are just phenomenal.

"If I was the fans I'd milk it, because of the desperation of last season and the horrible feeling of it and it's nice to give them something back for their efforts – for them and the players I'm absolutely delighted."

PROMOTION POINTS

⚽ The Canaries earned promotion one year ahead of when the club's directors had hoped to achieve Championship status.

⚽ Striker Grant Holt, the club's Player of the Year, hit 30 goals. The previous season he had been League Two's top scorer with 28 for Shrewsbury.

⚽ City got revenge by winning 5-0 at Colchester!

LEAGUE ONE FINAL TABLE

01	Norwich City	46	42	95
02	Leeds United	46	33	86
03	Millwall	46	32	85
04	Charlton Athletic	46	23	84
05	Swindon Town	46	16	82
06	Huddersfield Town	46	26	80
07	Southampton	46	38	73
08	Colchester United	46	12	72
09	Brentford	46	3	62
10	Walsall	46	-3	62
11	Bristol Rovers	46	-11	62
12	Milton Keynes Dons	46	-8	60
13	Brighton & Hove Albion	46	-4	59
14	Carlisle United	46	-3	58
15	Yeovil Town	46	-4	53
16	Oldham Athletic	46	-18	52
17	Leyton Orient	46	-10	51
18	Exeter City	46	-12	51
19	Tranmere Rovers	46	-27	51
20	Hartlepool United	46	-8	50
21	Gillingham	46	-16	50
22	Wycombe Wanderers	46	-20	45
23	Southend United	46	-21	43
24	Stockport County	46	-60	25

COUNTY CRACKERS!

NOTTS ACHIEVE THEIR AMBITION

The season began with a fanfare of massive promises, the arrival of Sven Goran Eriksson and former England defender Sol Campbell.

Fans were promised promotion to the Premier League within a few years and a Manchester City or Chelsea-style big-money revolution.

Sol managed one game. Sven departed. Managers changed... but County fans were still able to celebrate a goal fest and promotion as League Two champions.

The signing of Man City keeper Kasper Schmeichel, son of Peter, proved a very valuable acquisition – although he would later agree to rip up his lucrative contract so he could leave and also relieve County of the financial burden.

But perhaps the best bit of business was signing veteran goal machine Lee Hughes – you knew what was going to happen when he got a hat-trick on his debut!

The 33-year-old finished with 33 goals for the season, the first County player to reach the 30 landmark for 60 years.

The title-winning charge is even more remarkable when you look at the Magpies' management upheaval.

Sven and Ian McParland started the season as their management team, it changed to Hans Backe for seven weeks before Dave Kevan was appointed as caretaker until the end of the season - before Steve Cotterill took over in February until the end of the campaign!

PROMOTION POINTS

⚽ New arrival Karl Hawley (right) only scored three league goals for County, but they were vital.

⚽ Lee Hughes won the Manager's Player of the Year, Players' Player of the Year and the Golden Boot. Midfielder Ben Davies was the Supporters' Player of the Year.

⚽ Kasper Schmeichel broke an 80-year old club record by keeping 23 of the team's 25 clean sheets.

LEAGUE TWO FINAL TABLE

01	Notts County	46	65	93
02	Bournemouth	46	17	83
03	Rochdale	46	34	82
04	Morecambe	46	9	73
05	Rotherham United	46	3	73
06	Aldershot Town	46	13	72
07	Dagenham & Redbridge	46	11	72
08	Chesterfield	46	-1	70
09	Bury	46	-5	69
10	Port Vale	46	11	68
11	Northampton Town	46	9	67
12	Shrewsbury Town	46	1	63
13	Burton Albion	46	0	62
14	Bradford City	46	-3	62
15	Accrington Stanley	46	-12	61
16	Hereford United	46	-11	59
17	Torquay United	46	9	57
18	Crewe Alexandra	46	-5	55
19	Macclesfield Town	46	-9	54
20	Lincoln City	46	-23	50
21	Barnet	46	-16	48
22	Cheltenham Town	46	-17	48
23	Grimsby Town	46	-26	44
24	Darlington	46	-54	30

10

THINGS YOU NEED TO KNOW ABOUT...
JAMES MILNER

1. James Milner made his debut for Leeds in 2002 when he was just 16-years and 309 days! At the time, that made him the Premier League's second-youngest player ever. On December 26 that year he became the league's youngest-ever scorer.

2. He supported Leeds United as a youngster. His parents were both season tickets holders at Elland Road and he was a ball boy.

3. In July 2004, he transferred to Newcastle United when Sir Bobby Robson bought him for an initial £3.6m.

4. Milner later had a loan spell with Aston Villa before signing for them permanently in August 2008 for a staggering £12m – a fee that now seems a bargain!

5. This is one player you are more likely to see celebrating victories with milk rather than champagne, as Milner has never drunk alcohol.

6. He was in the same Leeds team as now-England team-mate Aaron Lennon, who was his room-mate during their time at Elland Road. Keeper Scott Carson was also in the squad.

7. Milner set a record for the number of appearances for England's Under-21 side with 46 caps to his name and nine goals.

8. It's no surprise that he runs almost non-stop from the start of a game to the final whistle as Milner was a long-distance runner at school where he also played football and cricket!

9. He was no mug at other subjects either and got 11 GCSEs before he joined Leeds. He had been on the clubs books since the age of ten.

10. Although he is mostly used wide midfield – on either side – Milner is also very effective when he is in the centre of the park. He can also operate up front, just behind the striker and has even played in defence! Nothing like being versatile!

IT'S A FACT...

Name:
James Philip Milner

Birth Date:
January 4, 1986

Birth Place:
Leeds

Position:
Midfielder

Clubs:
Leeds, Swindon
(loan), Newcastle,
Aston Villa

AVFC

PREPARED

IT'S A FUNNY OLD GAME...

OUR PHOTOGRAPHERS HAVE SNAPPED SOME GREATS SHOTS AT GAMES OVER THE PAST YEAR... HERE ARE JUST A FEW

Andrey Arshavin throws in the towel

Brighton fans test the new anti-seagull splatter outfits

Bendtner didn't see Barca's answer to Peter Crouch sneaking up on him...

"I know you have a bad head – but it shouldn't stop you scoring."

Blackburn knew if they could hypnotise David Dunne he might score a goal

It was rather cold at the Birmingham City game...

Park and Macheda knew someone had trumped – they just weren't sure who!

"Come on, you can't be serious about me wearing this shirt boss!"

Answers

Page 10-11 Brain teasers

Planet Football
A. Palacios **B.** Messi **C.** Kaka **D.** Eto'o
E. Henry **F.** Buffon **G.** Park **H.** Nelsen

Famous shirts

7 Eric Cantona **9** Shearer **10** Diego Maradona
14 Thierry Henry **23** Beckham **39** Nicolas Anelka

Page 32-33 Spot the Boss

Page 38-39,
Test your knowledge

Transfer tracker **Crouch** Portsmouth **Guthrie** Liverpool
Rodriguez Atletico Madrid **Tevez** Man United
Zhirkov CSKA Moscow **Obertan** Bordeaux

Ground Zero

Newcastle St. James' Park, 52,300
Arsenal Emirates, 60,400 **Doncaster Keepmoat** 15,200
Nottingham Forest City Ground 30,600
Man City Eastlands 48,000

Page 48-51 A-Z

A. Andrey Arshavin **B.** Jimmy Bullard **C.** Carlton Cole
D. Michael Dawson **E.** Eduardo **F.** Brad Friedel
G. Craig Gordon **H.** Henrique Hilario **I.** Isaiah Osbourne
J. Jonas Gutierrez **K.** Salomon Kalou **L.** Liam Lawrence
M. James McFadden **N.** Neville (Gary and Phil)
O. Nedum Onuoha **P.** Peter Crouch **Q.** Franck Queudrue
R. Jack Rodwell. **S.** Mark Schwarzer **T.** Fernando Torres
U. Matt Upson **V.** Jan Veneegor (of Hesselink)
W. Theo Walcott **X.** Xabi Alonso
Y. Ashley Young **Z.** Pablo Zabaleta

Page 54 Spot the Ball

Chile v
Switzerland
D5

Italy v New
Zealand
D6

Slovenia v
England
B3

USA v
Algeria
D7

Page 58 Whose pet?

Cisse - parrot **Owen** - horse
Mourinho - Yorkshire Terrier **Keane** - golden Labrador
Ireland - fish **Cole** - Bulldog